Pasta Artigiana

Nino Zoccali

Pasta Artigiana

SIMPLE *to* EXTRAORDINARY

photography by Nicky Ryan

MURDOCH BOOKS

This book is for
Luca and Krissoula

Introduzione
Introduction

La straordinarietà del cibo semplice
The extraordinariness of simple food

Quite a few years ago, when I was considerably younger than I am today, I opened my first restaurant in the Margaret River wine region in Western Australia with Russell Barr, an old childhood friend. We had both grown up in the small coastal city of Bunbury, close to this wonderful place. We loved the region; it was a renowned surfing coastline and we were both very eager surfers in those days. As restaurateurs, however, we were very inexperienced and had a lot to learn. But what we lacked in experience we definitely made up for in passion and enthusiasm. Russell looked after the front of house and I looked after the kitchen.

One day, not long after the opening of the restaurant, I received a phone call from my father advising me that he was coming to the restaurant with a group of people and that he would bring a good friend of his, a certain Swiss man by the name of Max Fehr. Max was a highly awarded chef and had successfully owned and operated restaurants for many years. His illustrious cooking career had also included opening restaurants and hotels all over the world and at the time he was still an international Olympic culinary judge. As you can imagine, I was young (25 years old), relatively inexperienced and extremely nervous about cooking for him.

As the date of my father's trip drew closer, I became almost paralysed with fear at the thought of what Max might order. Would it be the veal? After all, he was Swiss and the Swiss loved veal. Would it be the beef? The North West cod? The Fremantle sardines? The pork cutlets? Then I thought, 'Surely he is not going to order pasta, which is such a simple and relatively uninteresting option for someone like him.'

The evening of the dinner finally arrived, and when the order reached the kitchen, I was, to say the least, left in a state of shock. Max ordered, quite simply, a plate of fettuccine with neapolitan tomato sauce with basil, chilli and garlic. He couldn't have ordered a more basic dish and I have to say I felt slightly insulted.

Max ate the dish and then sent magnanimous compliments back to the kitchen. He told me that the pasta was as wonderful as Italian food could be and that I should be very proud of successfully carrying on such a magnificent tradition. He was also very interested to know how I made the sauce, how much olive oil I'd used, whether I used onions, the ratio of the ingredients and so on. I appreciated Max's compliments but thought, 'That's not what restaurant food should look or taste like.'

At the end of the evening service, when most of the patrons had left the restaurant, I decided to cook myself the same dish. And with just one small mouthful I was reminded of the thousands of times I had eaten this and many other simple pasta dishes, simple food that delivers such extreme satisfaction because it is cooked with love, care, passion and often obsession. I thought to myself, 'A simple lesson in the extraordinariness of simple food.' If it is done very well—with the right flavour and texture, the sauce made from the ripest tomatoes, the pasta cooked perfectly *al dente*—a simple plate of *pasta alla napoletana* (and let's face it, it doesn't get simpler than that) can, and indeed should be, a truly delightful experience.

On this particular evening I learnt a very important lesson, one that has defined my cooking philosophy and stayed with me for my entire career—that the quintessential cornerstone of great Italian cooking is simplicity, quality and, above all else, flavour.

Since that evening, I have cooked this simple dish, or close versions, for a multitude of people: heads of state, prime ministers, respected business leaders,

Formula One racing car drivers, famous musicians, actors, artists, sports stars and so on. According to Arrigo Cipriani, of Venice's iconic Harry's Bar, 'Spaghetti al pomodoro is one of those basic recipes that every Italian restaurant should be able to do well. In fact, you can use the dish to judge a restaurant.' I couldn't agree more.

Indeed, simple can be stunning if it is done well. It is no accident that spaghetti bolognaise—the anglicised version of *spaghetti con ragù*—has colonised much of the culinary Western landscape. While the pasta bolognaise you find outside of Italy may vary significantly from what you get in Bologna, it is remarkable that this dish is the most popularly eaten meal in Australia. And six out of every ten adults in the UK claim to be able to make a bolognaise sauce without a recipe!

But don't be fooled. In Italian cooking, 'simple' doesn't really mean 'simple'. It can mean 'quick', but it only means 'simple' once you know what you are doing. And it nearly always means regional. In the Bologna region alone there are hundreds of recorded variations of the bolognaise ragù. Many years have gone into perfecting regional pasta dishes where traditions are strong and meaningful. Growing up in my family, it took at least three people to test whether the pasta was *al dente* before serving it. Similarly, I believe I could write a novella just on the ripeness and variety of tomatoes used for tomato sauce. With Italian food, like any great provincial food, simple things are not simple if you want to do them well, and pasta is a very good case in point, which is why practice and learning correct techniques will see markedly better results.

It is believed that the tradition of making and eating pasta is over 7000 years old. It was either the Ancient Greeks or the Etruscans who first worked out how to make pasta, just before the Arabs discovered the significant benefits it brought as a 'transportable food'. But if the Italians didn't invent pasta, they have certainly turned it into a fine art over a long period of time. And they have developed a fine art out of virtually nothing. Growing up, my mother would often

say to me, 'The thing about Italian cooking is that it creates amazing things out of very little.'

I have witnessed this through my whole life, first from my father, aunties and uncles who—like generations of other Italian emigrants—left their beloved land to create better lives for themselves and their children. And it is ironic that while they left behind a life of abject poverty, they took with them culinary magic, the 'alchemy of flavour'.

The truth in my mother's statement is really a window into understanding how pasta, like most Italian cuisine, has evolved out of poverty or *la cucina povera*, and how it ties together an obsession with flavour that spans the whole of Italy, no matter what the region. There is nothing more ubiquitous in Italian food, in any corner of the country, than flavoursome pasta dishes. Nothing more economical can support the range of nutrient-rich ingredients that come from the different microclimates that span this great peninsula and its islands. Quite simply, there is nothing more Italian than pasta.

This ability to create amazing things out of very little is evidenced all over Italy, whether it is in the plethora of tomato and olive oil-based dishes of the south, the wonderful egg pasta dishes of central and northern Italy, border-region dishes such as *cuscus* from Trapani in Sicily or the Austrian-influenced dumplings found in places such as the Alto Adige.

Italy is a land of great contrasts and diversity, and in this book I have endeavoured to present a kaleidoscope of regional pasta dishes for you to savour and enjoy. The recipes are presented with full acknowledgment of historical context and I have attempted to honour age-old tradition whilst blending developments from the current era. Some recipes are simply 100 per cent Nino Zoccali; they are dishes that I have developed over many years of cooking in restaurants, talking and cooking with family, and travelling and researching in Italy.

I hope you enjoy the recipes in this book and that they give you as much pleasure as they have given me.

Nino Zoccali

Pasta Asciutta

Dried Pasta

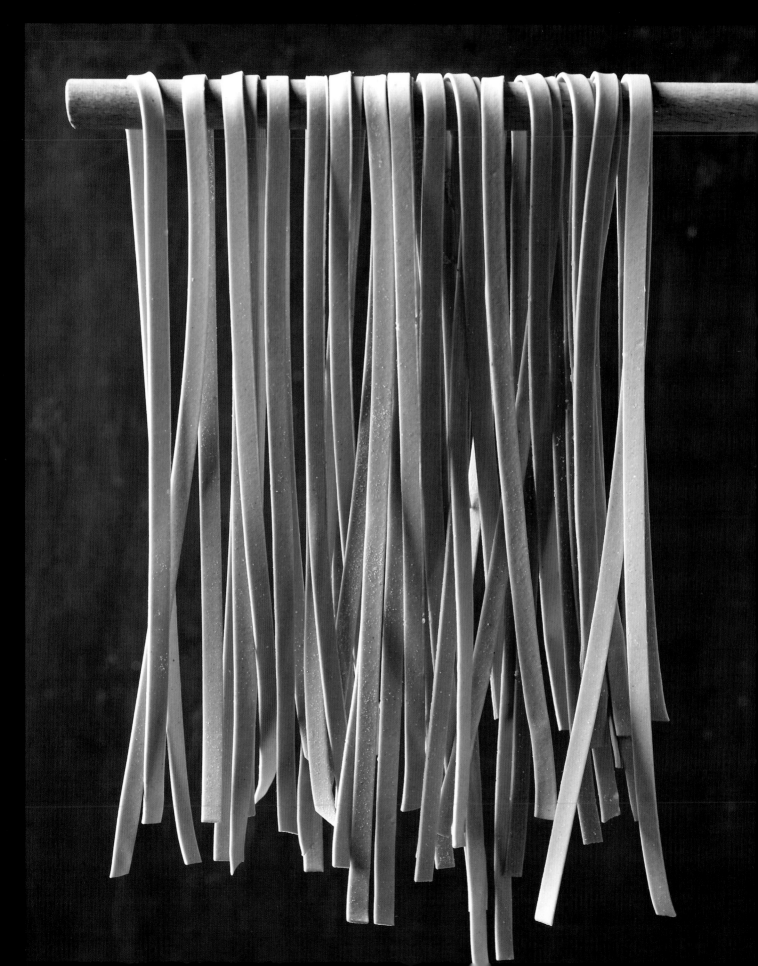

Il regno del sud
The domain of the south

Southern Italians have traditionally eaten more dried pasta than central and northern Italians. In fact, southern Italians don't even use the word pasta but *pasta asciutta* (dried pasta) when referring to pasta. Growing up, I thought that the north–south 'pasta divide' had evolved because southern Italy was much poorer than northern Italy. Given that fresh pasta is generally made with eggs and dried pasta with water, I believed that cost was the main reason for this, and my conclusion was that fresh pasta made with eggs was better. I was mistaken.

In reality, it really comes down to the type and quality of flour used. Egg really only appears in pasta-making in certain regions of Italy as a result of necessity. It was introduced as a way to successfully make pasta using plain flour rather than semolina flour (made from hard durum wheat). Plain flour does not work very well when it comes to making pasta with water alone, particularly if you are intending to dry it, as the pasta has less protein in it than hard durum wheat flour. Egg increases the protein in the dough and helps plain flour pasta remain intact and not become brittle and fall apart. If you ever try to make dried pasta with plain flour using water instead of eggs, you will see very quickly how the pasta is rendered virtually unusable as soon as it dries.

Historically, an abundance of high-quality hard durum wheat and ideal climatic conditions—such as coastal maritime breezes in places like Naples and Sicily—drove the development of the dried pasta industry in southern Italy. The relative cheapness of dried pasta and its marvellous versatility saw it become central to the southern Italian diet.

Even though northern Italy now dominates the production of dried pasta (Parma boasts the world's largest dried pasta producer), its consumption still tends towards southern styles of cooking. Additionally, a large internal migration process from southern to northern Italy through the period of the Italian post-war industrial revolution, along with the explosion of communications and media, have accentuated this.

Nowadays, it is no more difficult to find *linguini alle vongole* in a restaurant in Milan as it is to find it in Naples. And if there was a national Italian dish, *spaghetti al pomodoro* (spaghetti with tomato sauce) would have to come close to winning the prize. Like the ever-present *ragù di carne* (meat sauce), every region in Italy has a version of it or has incorporated it into its repertoire of regularly eaten dishes. This is significant in a place with such strong regional culinary heritage. Traditions tend to die slowly in Italy, and if they are strong, full of flavour and high in quality, they simply migrate! For obvious reasons, the dishes in this section are greatly influenced by the south.

Spaghettini della mamma con pollo e rosmarino

Mum's spaghetti with braised chicken thigh, tomato & rosemary sauce

Serves 6

This is a Zoccali family classic that is particularly popular with my nephews Nathan and Anton and niece Stella. The dish does, however, cause some debate in the family as opinions vary with respect to the ideal size of spaghetti that goes best with this sauce. I think this is a personal preference, but my favourite is very thin spaghetti (spaghettini).

Traditionally, my mother would braise the chicken thighs in the sauce and then remove them to be served as a main course after a pasta entrée. The sauce would be stirred through the pasta and served with lots of freshly grated parmesan or pecorino cheese. This recipe, however, calls for the chicken to be pulled apart and returned to the sauce before serving with the pasta. This is a good way to eat the dish if it is a quick meal. On the other hand, if you are making it for Sunday lunch and you have more time, then serving the meat as a second course with a lovely salad is a great way to eat it. The sauce will be flavoursome enough to carry the pasta if you plan to do it that way. Fresh chilli is a very Calabrian addition and an optional extra for the dish.

75 ml (2¼ fl oz) extra virgin olive oil

1 medium onion, chopped

1 garlic clove, finely chopped

400 g (14 oz) organic chicken thigh fillets

fine sea salt, to taste

freshly ground black pepper, to taste

400 ml (14 fl oz) good-quality tomato passata (puréed tomatoes)

1 rosemary sprig

1 bay leaf

chicken broth (page 185) or water, if needed for topping up braise

600 g (1 lb 5 oz) good-quality dried spaghettini

freshly grated Parmigiano Reggiano cheese, to serve

To make the sauce, heat half of the extra virgin olive oil in a saucepan over low–medium heat and add the onion and garlic. Cook gently until they become translucent. In a separate saucepan, heat the remaining extra virgin olive oil over medium heat and add the chicken thighs. Season with sea salt and black pepper. Brown the thighs turning them as you go, taking care not to burn the meat. Add the browned chicken thighs and the oil from cooking to the onion and garlic, then add the tomato passata, rosemary and bay leaf. Raise the heat and slowly simmer for approximately 1 hour or until the meat begins to fall apart. Top up with chicken broth or water, if necessary. Set aside to cool. Once cool, take out the chicken pieces and pull them apart into bite-sized pieces before putting them back into the sauce. This sauce is great made a day or two in advance.

For the pasta, simply cook the spaghettini in abundant salted boiling water until *al dente*. At the same time, reheat the chicken and tomato sauce. When cooked, strain the pasta and return to the pot. Add the sauce and toss. Season with more sea salt and black pepper, if required, and serve immediately with lots of freshly grated Parmigiano Reggiano cheese.

Penne con 'nduja stagionato e pomodoro
Penne with Calabrian 'nduja sausage & tomato

Serves 6

2½ tablespoons extra virgin olive oil

1 small onion, finely diced

1 garlic clove, finely chopped

1 thyme sprig, picked

200 g (7 oz) 'nduja sausage, to be treated similarly to mince (ground) meat (see Note)

2½ tablespoons dry white wine

500 ml (17 fl oz/2 cups) good-quality tomato passata (puréed tomatoes)

fine sea salt, to taste

600 g (1 lb 5 oz) good-quality dried penne

freshly grated pecorino cheese, to serve

Slowly heat the extra virgin olive oil in a saucepan over low heat and add the onion, then the garlic and thyme. Slowly cook until they soften and become translucent. Add the 'nduja sausage, breaking it up with the back of a spoon, and continue to cook for a further 5 minutes before deglazing with the white wine. Cook until almost all the wine has evaporated then add the tomato passata. Season with the sea salt and slow-cook for 1–2 hours. Set aside. Cook the pasta in abundant salted boiling water until *al dente* and drain. Combine with the sauce and add more salt if required. Serve with lots of freshly grated pecorino cheese.

NOTE: *'Nduja is a 'spreadable' and usually very spicy Calabrian salami that is rapidly gaining popularity around the world. The precise methods of production and ingredients can vary significantly, but all versions are characterised by the inclusion of a lot of chilli and a very strong, albeit dried chilli/capsicum (pepper) flavour. The drier, seasoned versions of this product will suit this recipe better, but any form of 'nduja will work well.*

Linguine allo zafferano con calamarettini e radicchio

Saffron linguine with baby bottle squid & radicchio

Serves 6

600 g (1 lb 5 oz) baby bottle squid
  with tentacles, cleaned, beaks
  and eyes removed
600 g (1 lb 5 oz) good-quality dried
  saffron linguine
100 g (3½ oz) radicchio leaves
  (approximately 5 leaves), cut into
  1 cm (½ inch) square pieces
  (see Note)
2½ tablespoons extra virgin olive oil
fine sea salt, to taste
freshly ground black pepper, to taste
3 small garlic cloves, finely chopped
2½ tablespoons dry white wine

Firstly, make sure the squid are as dry as possible. Cook the pasta in abundant salted boiling water until *al dente*. One minute before draining the pasta, add the radicchio to the boiling pasta pot. About 3 minutes before the pasta is cooked, heat half of the extra virgin olive oil in a large deep-sided saucepan over high heat until it just begins to smoke. Quickly add the squid to the pan and season with the sea salt and black pepper. Turn the squid over and then add the garlic. Cook for a further 30 seconds before adding the white wine to the pan. Cook for a minute or until almost all the wine has evaporated. Take care not to overcook the squid as it can become tough very quickly. Try to use high heat and cook for the shortest time possible. Drain the pasta and radicchio and combine with the squid, garlic and wine in the pan. Add the remaining extra virgin olive oil and mix well. Serve the pasta immediately.

NOTE: *A smaller quantity of radicchio can be used in this recipe as it is a very bitter vegetable and should be used according to taste.*

Strozzapreti con gamberi

Strozzapreti with king prawns, minced calamari, tomato, taggiasca olives & chilli

Serves 6

This is a dish that I put on the menu at Otto Ristorante on Sydney Harbour when we opened it over a decade ago, just before the Sydney Olympics. I believe it is the only dish from that era that is still on the menu—a testament to how wonderful the flavours are.

100 ml (3½ fl oz) extra virgin olive oil

1 small leek, diced

100 g (3½ oz) raw calamari, minced

150 ml (5 fl oz) dry white wine, such as Pinot Grigio or Vermentino

400 ml (14 fl oz) good-quality tomato passata (puréed tomatoes)

garum (fermented fish sauce), to taste

freshly ground black pepper, to taste

600 g (1 lb 5 oz) good-quality dried strozzapreti

18 medium-sized green prawns (shrimp), peeled and deveined

1 teaspoon finely sliced red chilli

1 garlic clove, finely chopped

18 taggiasca (ligurian) olives, pitted

1 tablespoon finely chopped flat-leaf (Italian) parsley

Heat half of the extra virgin olive oil in a saucepan over low heat and add the leek and calamari. Sweat until the leek and calamari begin to caramelise and change colour. Take care not to do this too quickly as the idea is to develop a rich flavour through doing this slowly. Add 100 ml of the white wine to deglaze and cook until the wine has all but evaporated. Add the tomato passata and slowly bring to the boil. Season with the garum to the desired level of saltiness and the black pepper. Once the sauce has reached boiling point, lower the heat, cover and slow-cook for at least 1 hour. Check and stir periodically to prevent the sauce sticking to the bottom of the pan and burning. Set aside.

For the pasta, simply bring abundant salted water to the boil and cook the pasta until it is *al dente*. Strain the pasta and return to the pan.

In a large saucepan, heat the remaining extra virgin olive oil over high heat until it is just starting to smoke. Add the prawns, chilli and garlic. Turn the prawns, add the remaining white wine and cook until the wine evaporates. Add the cooked prawns, garlic and chilli and taggiasca olives to the tomato and calamari sauce and mix through. Add the sauce to the pasta. Adjust seasoning by adding further garum, if desired. Serve with the chopped parsley.

Bavette nere con vongole e zucchine

Squid ink bavette with clams & zucchini

Serves 6

500 g (1 lb 2 oz) clams (vongole)
100 ml (3½ fl oz) extra virgin olive
    oil, plus extra, to serve (optional)
135 g (4¾ oz) zucchini (courgette),
    cut into 1 cm (½ inch) dice
fine sea salt, to taste
freshly ground black pepper, to taste
600 g (1 lb 5 oz) good-quality dried
    squid ink bavette
1 small garlic clove, finely chopped
100 ml (3½ fl oz) dry white wine
2 tablespoons chopped flat-leaf
    (Italian) parsley

If they haven't been purged, place the clams in a solution of cool water and sea salt for several hours or overnight in a cool part of the house (if you refrigerate them, they'll close up and won't 'spit out' the sand). Use 30 g (1 oz) salt to each litre (35 fl oz/4 cups) of water. Drain and set aside.

Heat half of the extra virgin olive oil in a frying pan over medium–high heat until just before it begins to smoke and add the zucchini. Season with the sea salt and black pepper and cook until the zucchini is tender, continuously turning the pieces so that they brown but don't burn. Set aside. Cook the pasta in abundant salted boiling water until *al dente* and drain.

About 2–3 minutes before the pasta is cooked, heat the remaining extra virgin olive oil in a separate large saucepan until it just begins to smoke and carefully add the clams. Make sure the clams have been well drained of water before adding them to the pan otherwise you may get unwanted flames. Add the garlic and cook for about 30 seconds before adding the white wine. Cook until all the clams have opened and the alcohol is cooked out of the wine (when the sauce no longer tastes bitter). Set aside for a minute. Drain the pasta, add to the clams with the zucchini and combine. Season with a little more sea salt and black pepper and add more extra virgin olive oil if desired (I add lots). Mix the chopped parsley through the pasta and serve immediately.

Spaghetti al peperoncino con aglio, olio e prezzemolo
Chilli spaghetti with garlic, olive oil & Italian parsley

Serves 6

This is another simple, classic and super-quick dish that I never get tired of. We serve it in Caffè Pendolino, where we also make the dried chilli pasta in-house. This recipe is different from the traditional version, which calls for regular dried pasta and the addition of fresh or dried chilli, but both ways are great. The recipe below is a good guide, but you can use your own discretion with the quantity of the ingredients.

600 g (1 lb 5 oz) good-quality dried
   chilli spaghetti
150 ml (5 fl oz) extra virgin olive oil
   (see Note)
1 small garlic clove, thinly sliced
1 medium-heat long red chilli, sliced
   (optional)
2 tablespoons chopped flat-leaf
   (Italian) parsley
fine sea salt, to taste
freshly ground black pepper, to taste
freshly grated pecorino cheese,
   to serve

Cook the pasta in abundant salted boiling water until *al dente* and drain. As you are draining the pasta, heat half of the extra virgin olive oil in a saucepan over medium–high heat. Just before it begins to smoke, quickly add the garlic and chilli, if using, and stir a couple of times with a wooden spoon before removing the pan from the heat, taking care not to burn either the garlic or the chilli. Add the pasta to the garlic, chilli and oil and then stir in the parsley. Season with the salt and black pepper and serve the pasta immediately with lots of freshly grated pecorino cheese and the remaining extra virgin olive oil.

NOTE: *You can add a little of the pasta's cooking water to the sauce to reduce the quantity of oil required.*

Rigatoni con la pancia di tonno, carciofini e olive verdi di Sicilia

Rigatoni with tuna belly, baby artichokes, tomato, olives & chilli

Serves 6

2½ tablespoons extra virgin olive oil

2 garlic cloves, finely chopped

4 anchovy fillets, chopped

4 medium roma (plum) tomatoes, diced

24 green Sicilian olives, pitted and cut in half

fine sea salt, to taste

freshly ground black pepper, to taste

600 g (1 lb 5 oz) good-quality dried rigatoni

24 whole baby artichokes, cooked and peeled (see Note)

400 g (14 oz) fresh tuna belly, cut into 2 cm (¾ inch) dice

1 medium-heat long red chilli, sliced (optional)

To make the sauce, heat half of the extra virgin olive oil in a large saucepan over medium–high heat and add the garlic and anchovy. Cook for a few seconds before adding the tomato and olives. Season with a little of the sea salt and black pepper, cook for 10 minutes and then set aside. Cook the pasta in abundant salted boiling water until *al dente*. About 2–3 minutes before the pasta is cooked, reheat the tomato, anchovy and olive sauce and add the cooked baby artichokes and then the tuna belly pieces, taking care not to overcook the tuna pieces. The idea is to cook them so that they are still slightly pink inside. Drain the pasta, add to the sauce and toss adding the remaining extra virgin olive oil and the chilli, if using. Season with sea salt and black pepper, if required, and serve immediately.

NOTE: *To prepare the artichokes, trim the stalks by about 6 cm (2 ½ inches). Cook them whole in a saucepan of salted boiling water with a little strained lemon juice until cooked when tested with a skewer. Strain and cool. Then peel and discard the hard outer leaves, peel the stem and trim the top.*

Fettuccine di barbabietole con olive nere

Beetroot fettuccine with black olives & fresh goat's cheese

Serves 6

6 brown pickling onions
20 baby beetroot (beets)
2 litres (70 fl oz/8 cups) water
250 ml (9 fl oz/1 cup) white wine
250 ml (9 fl oz/1 cup) white wine vinegar
1 teaspoon fine sea salt
1 teaspoon sugar
3 tablespoons extra virgin olive oil
14 dried black olives, pitted and cut in half
600 g (1 lb 5 oz) good-quality dried beetroot fettuccine (See Note)
2 tablespoons roughly chopped flat-leaf (Italian) parsley
fine sea salt, to taste
freshly ground black pepper, to taste
fresh milanese or piedmontese soft fresh goat's cheese, to taste

To make the sauce, you must cook the onions and beetroot separately. For the onions, simply boil them in their skins in salted boiling water until they are just cooked all the way through. Take care not to overcook them. You can check this with a skewer during the cooking process. When they are ready, strain them and allow them to cool before carefully peeling and cutting them into quarters. For the beetroot, trim the tops to 2 cm (¾ inch), scrub the beetroot, then place in a saucepan with the water, white wine, vinegar, salt and sugar. Cook for 45–60 minutes until they are just cooked all the way through. Set aside to cool. Once cooled, peel each beetroot and halve or quarter them depending on the size of each beetroot. The idea is to have bite-sized pieces. Once cut, put the beetroot pieces back into the cooking liquor until ready to use.

When you are ready to cook and serve the pasta, heat half of the extra virgin olive oil in a frying pan over medium–high heat. When hot, add the beetroot, quartered onions and black olives and cook for a few minutes so that they caramelise. The onions should become nicely browned. Add approximately 100 ml (3½ fl oz) of the beetroot cooking liquor to deglaze the pan.

Cook the pasta in abundant salted boiling water until *al dente*. Strain the pasta, return to the warm pot and then toss the sauce through the pasta, adding the chopped parsley and remaining extra virgin olive oil. Season with the sea salt and black pepper, to taste. Serve with the fresh milanese goat's cheese crumbled on top.

NOTE: *If you can't find dried beetroot fettuccine, you can replace it with regular dried fettuccine.*

Loane con fave secche e fave fresche

Pugliese tagliatelle with fresh & dried fava beans, salted dried ricotta, parsley, mint & basil

Serves 6

For those who have never heard of this dish, it is an unusual, regional, peasant-style pasta. It is very simple—and I think it is great. When making the dish, keep in mind that the dried fava bean purée will thicken and dry very quickly once all the ingredients are combined, so it is important to serve the dish as quickly as possible once it is cooked. Feel free to increase the quantity of salted ricotta served on the dish, and you can likewise use more chilli and drizzle additional extra virgin olive oil at the end.

20 large fresh broad (fava) beans

300 g (10½ oz) dried broad (fava) beans, soaked overnight and drained

750 ml (26 fl oz/3 cups) vegetable broth (page 187) or chicken broth (page 185)

fine sea salt, to taste

500 g (1 lb 2 oz) good-quality dried loane (or tagliatelle)

200 ml (7 fl oz) extra virgin olive oil

2 garlic cloves, 1 clove sliced and 1 clove finely chopped

dried chilli flakes, to taste

3 flat-leaf (Italian) parsley sprigs, finely chopped

6 mint leaves, finely chopped

6 sweet basil leaves, finely chopped

100 g (3½ oz/1 cup) freshly grated Parmigiano Reggiano cheese

freshly ground black pepper, to taste

150 g (5½ oz) grated ricotta salata (salted dried ricotta cheese), to serve

Pod the broad beans then blanch in a saucepan of rapidly boiling salted water, drain and refresh in iced water. Peel and set aside.

Peel the skins of the soaked dried broad beans then place in a medium-sized saucepan and cover with vegetable or chicken broth. Season with the sea salt and cook slowly for about 1 hour or until the beans begin to fall apart. Add additional water during the cooking process if required. Pass the mixture through a food mill or blend in a food processor to make a smooth purée. Cook the pasta in abundant salted boiling water until *al dente*. Add the fresh broad beans to the pasta 1 minute before draining. After draining, return to the pot. Add the broad bean purée to the pasta and fresh broad beans.

In a separate saucepan, heat half of the extra virgin olive oil and add the sliced garlic. Cook for a few seconds and set aside for a minute before adding to the pasta and broad bean purée. Add the chilli flakes, herbs, chopped garlic and remaining extra virgin olive oil. Incorporate into the pasta and broad bean purée with the freshly grated Parmigiano Reggiano cheese. Season with the sea salt and black pepper. Serve immediately with grated ricotta salata.

Maccheroni alla norma

Maccheroni with tomato & eggplant sauce

Serves 6

Norma *is a famous opera written by Sicilian composer Vincenzo Bellini. It is said that Italian writer and poet Nino Martoglio was so delighted with this dish that he compared it to the great opera, hence the name* pasta alla norma.

1 medium–large eggplant (aubergine)

fine sea salt, to taste

2 tablespoons extra virgin olive oil, plus extra for shallow-frying the eggplant

1 small onion, finely diced

1 garlic clove, finely chopped

500 g (1 lb 2 oz) peeled and deseeded ripe tomatoes, chopped

12 sweet basil leaves

600 g (1 lb 5 oz) good-quality dried long maccheroni

100 g (3½ oz) ricotta salata (salted dried ricotta cheese)

freshly grated Parmigiano Reggiano or pecorino cheese, to serve

Peel the eggplant and cut into 2 cm (¾ inch) cubes. Place in a bowl and lightly douse with the sea salt. Mix the salt evenly through the eggplant and then place the eggplant into a colander for about 1 hour to allow the salt to draw out any bitter juices. Pat the pieces dry with a tea towel (dish towel).

Slowly heat the extra virgin olive oil in a saucepan over low–medium heat. Add the onion and garlic and slowly cook until they are soft and translucent. Add the tomato and cook for about a further 15 minutes before adding half of the basil leaves. Set aside.

Fill a deep frying pan to approximately 1 cm (½ inch) deep with extra virgin olive oil and bring to medium–high heat. Pan-fry the eggplant cubes until completely cooked (soft right through the pieces). Take care to turn the eggplant pieces while cooking so as to avoid burning. Set aside.

Cook the pasta in abundant salted boiling water until *al dente*, strain and return to the pot. A few minutes before the pasta is cooked, combine the tomato sauce and eggplant and reheat. Check for seasoning (you shouldn't need any additional salt as the eggplant is already quite salty) and combine the tomato and eggplant sauce with the pasta. Grate or crumble the salted ricotta through the pasta. Tear up the remaining basil leaves and fold them through the pasta as well. Serve with lots of freshly grated Parmigiano Reggiano or pecorino cheese.

Bigoli integrali con sardine
Wholemeal bigoli with sardines

Serves 6

This dish is a staple in the Veneto region and comes in various forms. This version is one of the simplest, and my favourite. It is also the favourite dish of Pendolino sommelier Cristian Casarin, who grew up in a small town near Venice. Traditionally, the dish was made with home-cured freshwater sardines from lakes in or around the Veneto region. At the Pendolino and La Rosa restaurants, we cure our own sardines, and they are fantastic, although we have not been able to source freshwater sardines, only the saltwater type. Curing sardines is a great thing to do, but if you don't like the smell of fish, I would recommend avoiding the activity at all costs as the aroma will stay on your hands for several days. Yes, it is one of the 'favourite' jobs at the restaurants! Saltwater sardines are widely used in the dish in Italy and are a great substitute. The ratio of sardines and onion can be varied depending on personal preference. Cristian likes lots and lots of both sardines and onions, particularly onions. Some people also add tomato.

300 g (10½ oz) whole cured
   sardines in salt
100 ml (3½ fl oz) extra virgin
   olive oil, plus extra, to serve
2 medium onions, finely chopped
1 garlic clove, finely sliced
100 ml (3½ fl oz/⅓ cup) white wine,
   such as Pinot Grigio
600 g (1 lb 5 oz) good-quality dried
   wholemeal (whole-wheat) bigoli
   (see Note)
fine sea salt, to taste
freshly ground black pepper, to taste

Rinse the sardines to remove any excess salt. Pat dry and then debone. Heat the extra virgin olive oil in a large saucepan over medium–high heat. Add the onion and then the garlic approximately 5 minutes later. Cook the onion and garlic until they are completely cooked and soft. Add the sardine flesh and cook until the flesh begins to break up. Turn up the heat, add the white wine and cook until the wine has nearly completely evaporated. While the sardines and onion are cooking, stir vigorously to break up the sardine flesh to make a sauce. Cook the pasta in abundant salted boiling water until *al dente*. A few minutes before the pasta is cooked, reheat the sardine sauce. Add the pasta to the sardine sauce and toss, adding as much additional extra virgin olive oil as desired. Season with the sea salt and black pepper, if required, and serve immediately.

NOTE: *Bigoli are long, thick pasta tubes similar to bucatini. Traditionally, they were made with buckwheat flour, but nowadays they are more commonly made with wholemeal (whole-wheat) flour.*

Bucatini con baccalà e olive secche

Bucatini with slow-cooked salt cod, tomato & dried olive sauce

Serves 6

2½ tablespoons extra virgin olive oil, plus extra, to serve (optional)

1 medium onion, chopped

1 garlic clove, finely chopped

200 g (7 oz) skinless pin-boned baccalà (salt cod), soaked for at least 2 days (water needs to be changed twice daily), cut into 2 cm (¾ inch) cubes

1 teaspoon finely chopped hot chilli (optional)

12 dried black olives, pitted and cut in half

1 bay leaf

2½ tablespoons dry white wine

300 ml (10½ fl oz) good-quality tomato passata (puréed tomatoes)

600 g (1 lb 5 oz) good-quality dried bucatini

fine sea salt, to taste

freshly ground black pepper, to taste

2 tablespoons chopped flat-leaf (Italian) parsley

To make the sauce, heat the extra virgin olive oil in a saucepan over low–medium heat and add the onion and garlic. Cook gently until they become translucent. Raise the heat and add the salt cod, chilli, if using, olives and bay leaf. Cook for a few minutes before adding the white wine to deglaze the pan. Continue to cook until the wine has nearly completely evaporated then add the tomato passata. Simmer for 30 minutes or until the cod is tender and falling apart.

Cook the bucatini in abundant salted boiling water until *al dente*. At the same time, reheat the sauce. When cooked, simply strain the pasta, return to the pot and stir through the sauce. Season with the sea salt and black pepper if required. Add the parsley and more extra virgin olive oil, if desired. Serve immediately.

La gramigna con ragù modenese
Spinach pasta with modenese sauce

Serves 6

This recipe is inspired by a dish that I tasted in one of my favourite places to eat in Italy, Trattoria Ermes in Modena. It is one of the simplest and most memorable meals that I have ever eaten. Trattoria Ermes is a great 25-seat trattoria in one of the back streets of the city where you will find the most amazing traditional Modenese cooking. In this dish, ragù is simply at its best. We serve it in Caffè Pendolino in Sydney and it has become another iconic dish that will be very difficult to take off the menu. At Pendolino, we make a dried version of gramigna (wild weed) pasta in our dedicated pasta kitchen. Gramigna pasta may be difficult to find outside of Italy and can be substituted with spinach fettuccine or spinach tagliatelle, two other classic pastas used with ragù.

700 g (1 lb 9 oz) modenese sauce
   (page 190)
fine sea salt, to taste
freshly ground black pepper, to taste
600 g (1 lb 5 oz) good-quality dried
   gramigna pasta (or any other dried
   spinach pasta)
freshly grated Parmigiano Reggiano
   or pecorino cheese, to serve

Heat the modenese sauce in a small saucepan. Check seasoning and adjust with the sea salt and black pepper, to taste. For the pasta, simply bring abundant salted water to the boil and cook until it is *al dente*. Strain the pasta and return to the pot. Add the sauce and mix. Check seasoning again and serve with freshly grated Parmigiano Reggiano or pecorino cheese.

Spaghetti della zia Maria con costate di maiale
Zia Maria's pork rib spaghetti

Serves 6

My aunties zia Maria and zia Lidia are the best cooks in the world and I have included recipes in this book from both of them. Sadly, I couldn't include one from my zia Giovanna, who passed away many years ago. She was a fantastic cook and I still miss her and her cooking, particularly her wonderful cakes. This is a simple pasta classic from zia Maria who is a master of pasta, as well as many other dishes. If I ever write a book on roasted meats, she will feature very strongly, as will the amazing salads that come from my zio Quintino's garden.

This dish uses spare ribs, the secondary braising cut section of the rib, as opposed to the rib cutlet, a leaner roasting or grilling cut. Not surprisingly, Italian cooking does a lot with secondary cuts and it is interesting that in some parts of the world these ribs are called 'Italian ribs'. They are perfect for braising because meat close to the bone tends to be more flavoursome. Pork spare ribs also have lots of connective tissue that turns to a wonderfully unctuous and extremely flavoursome 'jelly' as it slowly cooks. Perfection!

100 ml (3½ fl oz) extra virgin olive oil

1 kg (2 lb 4 oz) pork spare ribs

fine sea salt, to taste

freshly ground black pepper, to taste

1 small brown onion, finely diced

2 garlic cloves, finely chopped

125 ml (4 fl oz/½ cup) white wine

750 ml (26 fl oz/3 cups) good-quality tomato passata (puréed tomatoes)

600 g (1 lb 5 oz) good-quality dried spaghetti

freshly grated Parmigiano Reggiano cheese, to serve

Heat the extra virgin olive oil in a saucepan over medium–high heat and seal the pork ribs in batches until brown. Season with the sea salt and black pepper, then remove and set aside. In the same saucepan, sauté the onion and garlic until translucent. Deglaze with the white wine and reduce until it has almost evaporated. Return the ribs to the pan and add the tomato passata. Cover and simmer for almost 2 hours, or until the ribs are tender. Remove the flesh from the bones and discard the bones.

Cook the pasta in abundant salted water until *al dente*, drain and stir through the sauce. Serve topped with freshly grated Parmigiano Reggiano cheese.

Tagliatelle verdi alla bolognese
Green tagliatelle with traditional bolognaise sauce
Serves 6

In Bologna, meat sauces are almost exclusively served with fresh pasta made from egg, or spinach and egg. Sometimes, however, fresh egg pasta is dried and used for the same purpose. The texture is not quite as soft, but it is still beautiful with the sauce. Dried egg pasta has become more and more popular because it is a quick and convenient way to have an egg pasta dish when you are time-poor and can't make your own pasta. Obviously, this sauce is wonderful with fresh spinach and egg pasta as well.

850 g (1 lb 14 oz) bolognaise sauce
  (page 194)
fine sea salt, to taste
freshly ground black pepper, to taste
600 g (1 lb 5 oz) good-quality dried
  spinach and egg tagliatelle
freshly grated Parmigiano Reggiano
  cheese, to serve

Heat the bolognaise sauce in a saucepan. Check seasoning and adjust with the sea salt and black pepper, to taste. Cook the pasta in abundant salted water until *al dente*. Drain the pasta, return to the pot and stir through the heated bolognaise sauce. Check seasoning again and finish with freshly grated Parmigiano Reggiano cheese.

Spaghetti alla napoletana
Spaghetti with neapolitan tomato sauce & basil
Serves 6

As mentioned in the introduction to this book, spaghetti alla napoletana *is one of the greatest pasta dishes you can eat—if it is done well. With something so simple, it's all about the quality of the ingredients. The tomatoes need to be at the very peak of ripeness, and, ideally, ripened on the vine. When making passata for tomato sauce, my father usually waits until past the peak of the tomato-producing season, when the tomato plant has dried out and the red tomatoes are the only thing left on the vines. This ensures that the natural sugar levels of the tomatoes are at their peak. If you make the passata this way, you can literally 'smell' the ripeness, and the sauce will be extraordinary.*

600 ml (21 fl oz) neapolitan tomato
 sauce (page 190)
600 g (1 lb 5 oz) good-quality dried
 spaghetti
fine sea salt, to taste
extra virgin olive oil, to taste
sweet basil leaves (optional)
freshly grated pecorino or Parmigiano
 Reggiano cheese, to serve

Heat the neapolitan sauce in a small saucepan. Cook the pasta in abundant salted boiling water until *al dente* and drain. Combine the sauce with the pasta and add more sea salt if required. Add as much extra virgin olive oil as desired (I add a lot). Sweet basil leaves can be added, if desired. Serve the pasta with lots of freshly grated pecorino or Parmigiano Reggiano cheese.

Pasta Fresca

Fresh Pasta

Il regno del nord
The domain of the north

Making fresh pasta has to be one of life's greatest pleasures. The simple process of turning a handful of basic ingredients into wonderful, golden, silky sheets of different pasta just makes you feel good. I have made fresh pasta with four-year-olds and with people who were close to 100. Everyone loves it!

Fresh pasta is made predominantly with egg and plain flour, so even if it is dried, the pasta is very different from dried pasta made with hard durum wheat semolina and water. The texture is generally much softer and the taste much richer. It is not supposed to be an *al dente* experience as the pasta is usually quite soft, even if undercooked.

As I often say, dishes made from both dried and fresh pasta can and should be special. In my opinion, it is hard for fresh pasta not to be special. Make some fresh egg tagliatelle, drop them into well salted boiling water, and cook. When ready, strain and toss them with a generous amount of both butter and freshly grated Parmigiano Reggiano cheese and you will have something very, very special. Add a little freshly sliced white truffle and it is no longer special, it is something so good that it is hard to describe. This could easily be my last meal. Wonderfully made fresh tagliatelle—even without the butter, cheese and truffle—taste pretty good. Fresh egg pasta is simply special!

There are infinite varieties of fresh egg pasta. The ones I use most often are saffron, stinging nettle, squid ink, chestnut flour and buckwheat flour (see pages 202–210). You'll find eight recipes for fresh pasta in the basics chapter.

In this section of the book, recipe inspiration is taken in large part from northern Italy. In the introduction to the section on dried pasta, I explained why this is the case. This is not to say that southern Italians don't make fresh pasta, they simply don't have the same historical relationship with it, and sauces from the centre and north of Italy tend to marry more harmoniously with fresh pasta. I have, however, included a few southern Italian fresh pasta family favourites as well.

Linguine con granchio al garum

Linguine with swimmer crab, tomato & garum sauce

Serves 6

100 ml (3½ fl oz) extra virgin olive oil

1 small leek, diced

1 garlic clove, finely chopped, plus
    extra ½ clove, finely chopped,
    if desired

100 ml (3½ fl oz/⅓ cup) dry white
    wine, such as Pinot Grigio or
    Vermentino

200 ml (7 fl oz) crustacean broth
    (page 189), reduced to
    100 ml (3½ fl oz)

500 ml (17 fl oz/2 cups) good-quality
    tomato passata (puréed tomatoes)

garum (fermented fish sauce), to taste
    (see Note)

freshly ground black pepper, to taste

600 g (1 lb 5 oz) fresh egg pasta
    dough (page 197), cut into linguine
    (page 200)

400 g (14 oz) cooked and picked blue
    swimmer crab meat

1 tablespoon finely chopped flat-leaf
    (Italian) parsley

Heat half the extra virgin olive oil in a saucepan over medium heat and add the leek and garlic. Sauté until they become translucent. Raise the heat to high, pour in the white wine and cook until the wine has evaporated. Add the reduced crustacean broth and tomato passata and season to taste with the garum and black pepper. Do not use any salt in this recipe. Bring to the boil then lower the heat and allow to simmer for about 10 minutes. Set aside.

For the pasta, simply bring abundant salted water to the boil then add the pasta. At the same time, reheat the sauce adding the cooked crab meat 1 minute before serving. Strain the pasta and combine with the sauce. Add the chopped parsley, remaining extra virgin olive oil and extra garlic, if desired, to the pasta, and combine well. Check for seasoning and add more garum if required. Serve immediately.

NOTE: *Garum (fermented fish sauce) can be substituted with Asian fish sauce.*

Tagliatelle di ortiche con sugo di capretto alla calabrese

Stinging nettle tagliatelle with braised goat & thyme sauce

Serves 6

2½ tablespoons extra virgin olive oil

1 small brown onion, diced

1 garlic clove, finely chopped

500 g (1 lb 2 oz) goat shoulder,
    cut into 2 cm (¾ inch) dice

fine sea salt, to taste

finely ground black pepper, to taste

700 ml (24 fl oz) good-quality tomato
    passata (tomato purée)

3 thyme sprigs

1 small bay leaf

water or beef broth (page 187),
    if needed during braise

600 g (1 lb 5 oz) stinging nettle fresh
    egg pasta dough (page 206),
    cut into tagliatelle (page 200)

freshly grated Parmigiano Reggiano
    or pecorino cheese, to serve

fresh crusty bread, to serve

Heat the extra virgin olive oil in a saucepan over medium heat and add the diced onion, garlic and goat meat. Season with the sea salt and black pepper and sauté until all are nicely browned. Add the tomato passata, thyme and bay leaf and bring to the boil. Lower the heat and simmer for 2–3 hours or until the goat meat has become 'fall-apart' tender. Add a little water or beef broth to the sauce throughout the cooking process if the sauce looks like it is becoming too reduced. Once cooked, simply set aside.

Bring abundant salted water to the boil and cook the pasta. With fresh egg pasta, the eating experience is different from dried pasta and the texture is much softer and not really *al dente*. Strain the pasta and stir through the sauce. Serve with lots of freshly grated Parmigiano Reggiano or pecorino cheese and fresh crusty bread.

Tagliolini neri con ostriche, caviale di salmone e tartufi

Black tagliolini with seared oysters, salmon caviar & white Alba truffle

Serves 6

24 freshly shucked large oysters

600 g (1 lb 5 oz) squid/cuttlefish ink fresh egg pasta dough (page 209), cut into tagliolini (page 200)

100 ml (3½ fl oz/) extra virgin olive oil

plain (all-purpose) flour, for dusting

½ teaspoon finely diced garlic

1 tablespoon finely chopped flat-leaf (Italian) parsley

1 tablespoon finely snipped chives

60 g (2¼ oz) fresh salmon caviar

18 thin slices fresh white Alba truffle

25 ml (½ fl oz) truffle oil (optional)

fine sea salt, to taste

freshly ground black pepper, to taste

This recipe involves a very quick cooking process. Depending on the thickness of the tagliolini, the pasta will take 2–5 minutes to cook and everything else will take only a matter of minutes to put together. You will need to cook the oysters and assemble the dish very quickly, so it is important that all the ingredients are on hand and ready to go.

Prepare the oysters by making sure they are as dry as possible. Dry them with a cloth or with kitchen paper. Drop the tagliolini into abundant salted boiling water. In the meantime, heat half of the extra virgin olive oil in a large heavy-based frying pan over very high heat. The pan needs to be very hot with the oil just at smoking point. Lightly dust the oysters with the plain flour and very quickly sear them in the hot pan. The idea is to crisp the outside of the oysters a little, but not overcook them in the middle. Turn the oysters quickly to brown all over then take them from the pan and place them in a large stainless steel bowl.

Once the pasta is cooked, drain and add to the oysters along with the garlic, parsley, chives, the remaining extra virgin olive oil, half of the salmon caviar, half of the shaved truffle and the truffle oil, if using. Season with the sea salt and black pepper and combine well. Serve immediately with the remaining salmon caviar and truffle.

Cappelli di preti con ragù di cinghiale
Priests' hats pasta with Calabrian wild boar sauce

Serves 6

600 g (1 lb 5 oz) fresh egg pasta
  dough (page 197)

fine semolina, for dusting

2½ tablespoons extra virgin olive oil

1 small brown onion, diced

2 garlic cloves, finely chopped

8 sage leaves

2 tablespoons chopped flat-leaf
  (Italian) parsley

350 g (12 oz) minced (ground) wild
  boar leg or shoulder (see Note)

350 g (12 oz) minced (ground) pork
  belly

fine sea salt, to taste

freshly ground black pepper, to taste

200 ml (7 fl oz) red wine

800 g (1 lb 12 oz) fresh roma (plum)
  tomatoes, peeled, deseeded and
  roughly chopped

1 teaspoon hot dried chilli flakes,
  plus extra, to serve (optional)

beef broth (page 187) or water,
  if needed

freshly grated pecorino cheese,
  to serve

To make the cappelli di preti pasta, take the fresh egg pasta dough and roll it out to sheets of no more than 1 mm (1/32 inch) in thickness. Cut the pasta sheets into 6.5 x 6.5 cm (2½ x 2½ inch) squares, then cut the squares diagonally in half to form two symmetrical triangles. Brush a little water on each fold of the bottom corners of the triangle and fold each of the corners to the centre to form the shape of a priest's hat. Lightly dust with semolina and set aside on baking trays lined with non-stick baking paper until ready to cook.

To make the sauce, heat the extra virgin olive oil in a saucepan over medium heat and sauté the diced onion, garlic, sage, half of the parsley and the boar and pork belly meat. Season with the sea salt and black pepper. Break up the minced meat with a spoon and sauté until all are nicely browned. Pour in the red wine and continue to cook until the wine has completely evaporated. Add the tomato, remaining parsley and chilli flakes. Cook slowly for at least 2 hours. You will need to add a little beef broth or water during the cooking process if the sauce looks like it is becoming too reduced.

Cook the pasta in abundant salted boiling water. When cooked, drain and mix with the sauce, adding a little of the pasta water. Serve hot with lots of freshly grated pecorino cheese. For those who like chilli, additional dried chilli flakes can be added to the dish at the end.

NOTE: *Order wild boar in advance from a specialist Italian butcher.*

Gnocchi alla dalmatina di Ino Kuvacic con ragù di bue

Ino Kuvacic's Dalmatian-style butter gnocchi with oxtail sauce

Serves 6

This gnocchi recipe comes from a dear friend and colleague—Ino Kuvacic. It is his grandmother's recipe from Dalmatia in Croatia and they are stunningly light and soft in texture. Ino and I are great friends and often discuss the striking similarities between Croatian and Italian food, and the strong Italian influence in the cooking of the Dalmatian region—a connection that extends back to the Venetian rule of Dalmatia, which lasted nearly 400 hundred years. These gnocchi are wonderful and can be served with a range of different sauces, as well as the oxtail sauce in this dish.

1 kg (2 lb 4 oz) oxtail, cleaned and trimmed of excess fat, cut roughly into 4 cm (1½ inch) long pieces

fine sea salt, to taste

freshly ground black pepper, to taste

100 ml (3½ fl oz) extra virgin olive oil

50 g (1¾ oz) pancetta, finely diced

1 garlic clove, chopped

1 onion, diced

1 celery stalk, diced

1 carrot, diced

100 ml (3½ fl oz) white wine

1 litre (35 fl oz/4 cups) chicken broth (page 185)

1 thyme sprig

600 g (1 lb 5 oz) Ino Kuvacic's Dalmation-style butter gnocchi (page 213)

90 g (3¼ oz) butter, chopped

50 g (1¾ oz/½ cup) freshly grated Parmigiano Reggiano, plus extra, to serve

To make the oxtail sauce, season the oxtail with the sea salt and black pepper, then heat half of the extra virgin olive oil in a saucepan over medium–high heat and cook the oxtail pieces until they are nicely browned.

In another saucepan, heat the remaining extra virgin olive oil over medium heat and cook the pancetta until crisp. Add the garlic, onion, celery and carrot. Cook for 10 minutes until the vegetables are tender. Add the white wine and oxtail and cook for 5 minutes until the wine has evaporated. Add the chicken broth and thyme and bring to the boil. Cover and simmer over low heat until the oxtail starts to come off the bone, approximately 2½–3½ hours. As the oxtail cooks, skim the fat from the top of the braising liquid. If the sauce is reducing too fast, you can add a little extra water or broth. Once cooked, take the oxtail from the sauce and let it cool down. Remove the meat from the bone and return it to the sauce. Reduce the sauce by a quarter.

Cook the gnocchi in abundant salted boiling water. As soon as they float to the surface they are ready and should be scooped out and placed in a serving bowl. Add the butter and freshly grated Parmigiano Reggiano cheese to thicken and enrich the oxtail sauce just before serving and spoon over the gnocchi. The extra Parmigiano Reggiano cheese can be grated over the gnocchi and sauce once it has been served.

Spaghetti con sugo di piccioni

Fresh spaghetti with squab, tomato & Greco Bianco white wine ragù

Serves 6

100 ml (3½ fl oz) extra virgin olive oil

1 small brown onion, diced

1 garlic clove, finely chopped

fine sea salt, to taste

freshly ground black pepper, to taste

3 medium-sized whole squabs

100 ml (3½ fl oz) Greco Bianco white wine or other dry southern Italian white wine

500 ml (17 fl oz/2 cups) good-quality tomato passata (puréed tomatoes)

500 ml (17 fl oz/2 cups) chicken broth (page 185)

1 small bay leaf

1 rosemary sprig

600 g (1 lb 5 oz) fresh egg pasta dough (page 197), cut into spaghetti (page 200)

freshly grated pecorino cheese, to serve

Heat half of the extra virgin olive oil in a saucepan over medium heat and add the onion and garlic. Season with the sea salt and black pepper and sauté until they are nicely browned. Set aside. In a separate saucepan, heat the remaining extra virgin olive oil and brown the whole squabs. Add the squabs to the pan with the onion and garlic, raise the heat, pour in the white wine and continue to cook until the wine has completely evaporated. Add the tomato passata, chicken broth, bay leaf and rosemary. Cook the sauce for up to 2 hours or until the meat is falling off the carcasses. When fully cooked, take the squabs from the sauce and let them cool down. Remove the meat from the bone and return the meat to the sauce.

For the pasta, simply bring abundant salted water to the boil and cook the pasta. When cooked, drain the pasta and stir through the sauce. Serve hot with lots of freshly grated pecorino cheese.

Pappardelle con ragù di vitello e maggiorana
Pappardelle with White Rocks Veal *&* marjoram ragù
Serves 6

This recipe owes its genesis to a Calabrian butcher by the name of Vincenzo Garreffa—a very close family friend and an extraordinary food innovator. I have featured his products on my menus over the years as he is particularly passionate about Italian butchery tradition and is a purveyor of the highest quality meat products available. Collaboration with him is particularly exciting. This dish, originally conceived for the first Pendolino menu and featuring Vince's wonderful White Rocks Veal, has become a signature menu item. When cooking this dish, make sure you stir the pot regularly as the flour coating on the meat tends to stick to the base, making it very easy to burn. While White Rocks Veal is a treat to use, this dish is fantastic with any good-quality veal product.

400 g (40 oz) veal chuck, trimmed and diced into 1–2 cm (½–¾ inch) cubes

fine sea salt, to taste

freshly ground black pepper, to taste

plain (all-purpose) flour, for dusting the meat

140 ml (4½ fl oz) extra virgin olive oil

1 small onion, finely diced

1 small carrot, finely diced

1 celery stalk, finely diced

1 garlic clove, finely diced

2 thyme sprigs, picked

1 rosemary sprig, picked

2 marjoram sprigs, picked

150 ml (5 fl oz) white wine

1 litre (35 fl oz/4 cups) beef broth (page 187)

600 g (1 lb 5 oz) fresh egg pasta dough (page 197), cut into pappardelle (page 200)

50 g (1¾ oz/½ cup) freshly grated Parmigiano Reggiano cheese, plus extra, to serve

50 g (1¾ oz) salted butter, chopped

Season the veal with the sea salt and black pepper and dust with the flour, taking care to shake off any excess. Heat 2 tablespoons of the extra virgin olive oil in a large saucepan over high heat and sauté the meat until it is golden. In a separate saucepan, heat the remaining extra virgin olive oil over medium–low heat and sauté the finely diced vegetables, garlic and herbs until lightly golden. Deglaze with the white wine and reduce by half. Add the cooked veal and beef broth. Season to taste. Bring to the boil and then turn down to a simmer and cook for approximately 2 hours or until the meat is tender and falling apart.

Bring abundant salted water to the boil and cook the pasta. With fresh egg pasta, the eating experience is different from dried pasta and the texture is much softer and not really *al dente*. Drain the pasta and add to the sauce. Stir through the freshly grated Parmigiano Reggiano cheese and butter to help thicken and enrich the sauce. Serve topped with additional Parmigiano Reggiano cheese.

Spaghetti alla chitarra con pesce d'acqua dolce

Fresh spaghetti alla chitarra with river fish & freshwater crayfish

Serves 6

9 medium-sized freshwater crayfish, such as marron

600 g (1 lb 5 oz) fresh egg pasta dough (page 197), cut into spaghetti (page 200)

100 ml (3½ fl oz) extra virgin olive oil, plus extra, to serve (optional)

300 g (10½ oz) freshwater river fish, such as barramundi or Murray River cod, skinless and diced

fine sea salt, to taste

freshly ground black pepper, to taste

3 garlic cloves, finely diced

2 tablespoons Italian salted capers, rinsed and drained

2 teaspoons sliced chilli

150 ml (5 fl oz) Pinot Grigio white wine

2 tablespoons chopped flat-leaf (Italian) parsley

NOTE: *It is important to be careful when cooking the crayfish as overcooking will make it rubbery.*

Prepare the freshwater crayfish by blanching them in salted boiling water for 1 minute before transferring them to an iced water slurry. This process partially cooks the crayfish (around and just under the shell), enabling them to be peeled in a raw product form. To peel, twist the middle fin of the tail shell and gently pull to remove the intestinal tract (it should come out easily). Next twist and remove the head. Then, using a pair of kitchen scissors, cut down the shell on the belly and slip the flesh from the shell. Cut the crayfish in half lengthways.

This recipe involves a cooking process that is very quick. Depending on the thickness, the spaghetti will take 3–6 minutes to cook, and the sauce will take only a matter of minutes. Once you have started cooking your pasta, you will need to cook the sauce straight away. It is important that all the ingredients are on hand and ready to go.

Drop the spaghetti into abundant salted boiling water. Next, heat half of the extra virgin olive oil in a large deep-sided frying pan over medium–high heat and add the crayfish and fish pieces (see Note). The pan needs to be very hot, with the oil just about at smoking point. Quickly season the crayfish and fish with the sea salt and freshly ground black pepper and then add the garlic, capers and chilli. While doing this, keep checking on how the spaghetti is going and drain it from the water as soon as it is cooked. Sauté the fish mix for a minute before pouring in the white wine. The pan should be very hot so that the wine reduces quickly. If you are not sure if your pan will be big enough or that it will retain enough heat, use two separate pans. Cook for a minute longer (until all the alcohol has been cooked out of the wine) before adding the cooked pasta to the pan. If the pasta is not quite ready, set the sauce aside for a minute until the pasta is cooked. This will not take long. Add the pasta to the sauce with the remaining extra virgin olive oil and the chopped parsley. Check for seasoning and stir the sauce through the pasta. Serve immediately. Additional extra virgin olive oil can be drizzled over the pasta, if desired.

Corsetti con ragù di coniglio
Ligurian coin pasta with braised rabbit sauce
Serves 6

These traditional Ligurian corsetti (ancient coins) are one of the most beautiful forms of pasta that exist. They are fun to make, too. The process of transforming basic pasta dough into wonderful pieces of edible art gives great satisfaction. In this recipe, I serve the corsetti with a traditional Ligurian rabbit ragù, while in Liguria they are often served with the more classic pesto alla genovese. *They are great with either sauce.*

600 g (1 lb 5 oz) fresh egg pasta
   dough (page 197)
100 ml (3½ fl oz) extra virgin olive oil
1 brown onion, diced
1 celery stalk, diced
1 carrot, diced
1 leek, diced
3 thyme sprigs
1 small bay leaf
1 garlic clove, finely chopped
fine sea salt, to taste
freshly ground black pepper, to taste
600 g (1 lb 5 oz) rabbit pieces on
   the bone
100 ml (3½ fl oz) dry white wine
500 ml (17 fl oz/2 cups) good-quality
   tomato passata (puréed tomatoes)
1 tablespoon tomato paste
   (concentrated purée)
500 ml (17 fl oz/2 cups) chicken broth
   (page 185)
freshly grated Sardinian pecorino
   or Parmigiano Reggiano cheese

Take the egg pasta dough and roll it into sheets of 1–2 mm (approx. ¹⁄₁₆ inch) thickness. Cut out the corsetti with a 6 cm (2½ inch) wide tool and stamp an insignia with the other side (to resemble an antique Roman coin).

Heat half of the extra virgin olive oil in a saucepan over low–medium heat and add the diced vegetables, thyme, bay leaf and garlic. Season the vegetables with the sea salt and black pepper and sauté until they soften and become translucent. Heat the remaining extra virgin olive oil in a separate saucepan over medium heat. Season the rabbit pieces and then cook them until they are nicely browned. Once the vegetables have softened, add the rabbit pieces and raise the heat. When hot, add the white wine and cook until the wine is almost completely evaporated. Next, add the tomato passata, tomato paste and chicken broth. Bring to the boil then simmer for at least 2 hours or until the rabbit meat is starting to fall off the bone. Once the meat has reached this point, take out the rabbit pieces and set aside to cool. Once cool, pick the rabbit meat from the bone and break into bite-sized pieces and return it to the sauce. Heat the rabbit sauce and set aside.

Cook the corsetti in salted rapidly boiling water for approximately 8 minutes or until completely cooked (more than *al dente*).

Spoon the rabbit sauce over the top of the corsetti pasta and serve immediately with lots of freshly grated Sardinian pecorino or Parmigiano Reggiano cheese.

Canederli di spinaci

Alto Adige-style spinach & bread dumplings with gruyère & Parmigiano Reggiano cheese

Serves 6–8

This dish is more commonly known by its Germanic name, knödel di spinaci, *rather than by its Italian counterpart,* canederli di spinaci. *Menus in Italy often use both versions to describe the dish. There is very little doubt that this dish is of strong German/Austrian origin. But over the course of history, it has become a very traditional dish of the Alto Adige, Trentino and other northern Italian regions. While not what we normally expect when eating pasta,* canederli *are wonderful and particularly great to eat in the middle of winter. I have eaten them in a little cabin in the middle of snow-covered mountains in the Alto Adige with my wife, son and sommelier, and I can't imagine a more fulfilling experience.*

120 g (4¼ oz) salted butter

1 medium onion, finely diced

fine sea salt, to taste

freshly ground white pepper, to taste

3 x 59 g (2¼ oz) free-range or organic eggs

freshly grated nutmeg, to taste

500 g (1 lb 2 oz) day-old bread, cut roughly into 1 cm (½ inch) square pieces

100 g (3½ oz/1 cup) grated gruyère cheese

3 tablespoons plain (all-purpose) flour

300 g (10½ oz) baby English spinach, boiled or steamed, then finely chopped and well drained

3 tablespoons full-cream (whole) milk

freshly grated Parmigiano Reggiano cheese, to taste

Put two-thirds of the butter in a saucepan over low heat and cook the onion until soft and translucent in colour. Season with the sea salt and white pepper and set aside to cool. Combine the eggs, nutmeg, bread, gruyère cheese, flour, cooled sautéed onion, spinach and milk to form a soft dough. Use a little more milk if required. Using wet hands, form the mixture into small dumplings (the size of large gnocchi). Cook in abundant salted boiling water for about 8–12 minutes. Drain and place on a hot or warm serving dish. Cover with the freshly grated Parmigiano Reggiano cheese, to taste. Heat the remaining butter in a small saucepan over high heat and cook until foaming and nut brown. Drizzle over the top of the cheese and dumplings and serve immediately.

Capellini di zafferano con aragosta

Saffron capellini with lobster & wild fennel sauce

Serves 6

1 x 800 g (1 lb 12 oz) rock lobster
  or crayfish (place in the freezer
  for 30 minutes first)
80 g (2¾ oz) butter
1 small leek, diced
1 garlic clove, finely chopped
40 g (1½ oz) salted baby capers,
  rinsed and drained
100 ml (3½ fl oz) dry white wine,
  such as Pinot Grigio or Vermentino
800 ml (28 fl oz) crustacean broth
  (page 189), reduced to 200 ml
  (7 fl oz)
200 ml (7 fl oz) good-quality tomato
  passata (puréed tomatoes)
3 wild fennel sprigs, picked, plus
  extra, to serve (optional)
fine sea salt, to taste
freshly ground black pepper, to taste
600 g (1 lb 5 oz) saffron fresh egg
  pasta dough (page 210), cut into
  capellini (page 200)
1 tablespoon finely chopped flat-leaf
  (Italian) parsley

Prepare the lobster by quickly boiling it for a short period, about 4 minutes. As soon as it is taken out of the boiling water, chill it down in an iced water slurry. This process partially cooks the lobster (around and just under the shell), enabling it to be peeled and used in a raw product form. Remove the head. Next remove the flesh from the shell by cutting along the underside with kitchen scissors and carefully removing the flesh from the shell. Next remove the intestinal tract by making a small incision along the back of the body and removing the tube. Slice the lobster into escalope pieces and set aside. The flesh inside the claws and legs will be fully cooked and can be removed and added to the escalope pieces.

Heat half of the butter in a medium saucepan over medium heat and add the leek, garlic and capers. Cook, stirring often, until the leek and garlic become translucent. Raise the heat to high, pour in the white wine and cook until the wine has evaporated. Add the reduced crustacean broth, tomato passata and wild fennel sprigs. Season with the sea salt and black pepper. Bring to the boil then lower the heat and allow to simmer for about 30 minutes. Set aside.

For the pasta, simply bring abundant salted water to the boil and add the pasta. While doing this, reheat the sauce, bringing it to a simmer and add the lobster escalopes and claw and leg flesh. Cook for approximately 2 minutes or until the lobster is just cooked. Add the parsley and melt the remaining butter through the sauce. Drain the pasta, return to the pot and add the lobster and sauce. Mix well and serve immediately. Garnish with extra picked wild fennel, if desired.

Späetzle con funghi di castagno

Späetzle with chestnut mushrooms

Serves 6

In Italy, as in Austria and Germany, späetzle *are not often served crisp as they are in this recipe. This is, however, a personal preference of mine. Parmigiano Reggiano cheese is another personal touch that gives the dish a distinctive Italian flavour and ties together all the ingredients. This dish is wonderful eaten by itself or as an accompaniment for meat and game.*

600 g (1 lb 5 oz) plain (all-purpose) flour

5 x 59 g (2¼ oz) free-range or organic eggs

fine sea salt, to taste

freshly grated nutmeg, to taste

220 ml (7½ fl oz) water

150 g (5½ oz) butter, chopped

extra virgin olive oil, to coat

SPÄETZLE SAUCE

2 tablespoons extra virgin olive oil

100 g (3½ oz) butter

2 small leeks, chopped

500 g (1 lb 2 oz) chestnut mushrooms (if in Europe, chiodini mushrooms can be used), only the larger ones sliced

fine sea salt, to taste

freshly ground black pepper, to taste, plus extra, to serve

150 ml (5 fl oz) white wine

2 tablespoons finely chopped flat-leaf (Italian) parsley

freshly grated Parmigiano Reggiano cheese, to serve

To make the späetzle, put the flour, eggs, sea salt, nutmeg and water in a large bowl. Whisk until it is completely smooth and there are no lumps. Let the dough rest for 1 hour, beating it from time to time.

Bring a large saucepan of salted water to the boil. Put 2–3 tablespoons of the dough into a potato ricer or späetzle press, if you have one, and push the dough into the water, cutting the pieces off with a sharp knife. They should be about 1–3 cm (½–1¼ inches) in length. As soon as they float to the surface of the water, they are ready. Scoop them out with a slotted spoon and place into a bowl of iced water. Repeat this process for the rest of the späetzle mixture. Strain the späetzle. Lightly coat with a little extra virgin olive oil and refrigerate. The oil will prevent the späetzle noodles from sticking to each other.

To make the sauce, heat the extra virgin olive oil and butter in a frying pan over medium heat. Sauté the leek until softened, then add the mushrooms. Increase the heat to high and sauté vigorously for about 4 minutes. Season the mixture with the sea salt and black pepper. Once the mushrooms are soft, deglaze with the white wine and continue to cook until the wine has evaporated then set aside. In a separate frying pan, heat the 150 g (5½ oz) butter over medium–high heat until foaming and cook the späetzle in batches for a few minutes until crispy. Return all the späetzle to the pan. Add the leek and mushroom mix and the parsley. Serve topped with the freshly grated Parmigiano Reggiano cheese and freshly ground black pepper.

Tagliatelle di farro con ragù di anatra

Spelt tagliatelle with duck & Sangiovese sauce

Serves 6

2½ tablespoons extra virgin olive oil

1 onion, diced

1 carrot, diced

1 celery stalk, diced

200 g (7 oz) pancetta, finely diced

1 garlic clove, finely chopped

fine sea salt, to taste

freshly ground black pepper, to taste

2 large duck marylands, skin removed

200 ml (7 fl oz) Sangiovese (Chianti) red wine

250 ml (9 fl oz/1 cup) good-quality tomato passata (puréed tomatoes)

300 ml (10½ fl oz) chicken broth (page 185)

1 small bay leaf

1 thyme sprig

50 g (1¾ oz) dried porcini mushrooms, double-washed in hot water and strained

1 rosemary sprig

600 g (1 lb 5 oz) spelt fresh egg pasta dough (page 203), cut into tagliatelle (page 200)

freshly grated Parmigiano Reggiano cheese, to serve

Heat half of the extra virgin olive oil in a saucepan over medium heat and add the onion, carrot, celery, pancetta and garlic. Season with the sea salt and black pepper and sauté until they are nicely browned. Be careful not to put in too much salt as the pancetta will be very salty. In a separate frying pan, heat the remaining extra virgin olive oil and brown the duck marylands. Transfer the duck to the pan with the sautéed vegetables. Raise the heat and pour in the red wine and continue to cook until the wine has completely evaporated, stirring occasionally. Add the tomato passata, chicken broth, bay leaf, thyme, porcini mushrooms and rosemary. Simmer over low heat for 2–2½ hours, adding extra chicken broth or water, if required, until the meat is falling off the bones. Take the duck from the sauce and let it cool down. Remove the meat from the bones and then return the meat to the sauce.

Cook the pasta in abundant salted boiling water. When cooked, drain the pasta and mix with the sauce and a little of the pasta water. Serve with lots of freshly grated Parmigiano Reggiano cheese.

Fettuccine di castagna con maiale e cavolo savoiardo
Chestnut flour fettuccine with pork & savoy cabbage

Serves 6

600 g (1 lb 5 oz) pork cheeks,
    trimmed and cleaned of all fat
250 ml (9 fl oz/1 cup) Chardonnay,
    reduced to 170 ml (5½ fl oz/⅔ cup)
1 onion, finely diced
1 leek, finely diced
1 celery stalk, finely diced
1 carrot, finely diced
1 rosemary sprig
4 sage leaves
700 ml (24 fl oz/2¾ cups) vegetable
    broth (page 187)
1 bay leaf
fine sea salt, to taste
freshly ground black pepper, to taste,
    plus extra, to serve
½ savoy cabbage, cored and roughly
    chopped
300 g (10½ oz) chestnut fresh egg
    pasta dough (page 202), cut into
    fettuccine (page 200)
50 g (1¾ oz) butter, chopped
freshly grated Parmigiano Reggiano
    cheese, to taste

Preheat the oven to 150°C (300°F/Gas 2). Place all the ingredients, except the savoy cabbage, pasta and butter, into a roasting tin. Cover with a cartouche (see Note), wrap the tin tightly in foil and bake for 2 hours or until the meat is falling apart. Remove from the oven and allow to cool. Break the meat into bite-sized pieces and return to the roasting tin. Remove the rosemary sprig and bay leaf and discard. Blanch the cabbage in salted boiling water and add to the roasting tin.

Cook the pasta in abundant salted boiling water. This will only take about 3–4 minutes. Drain and combine with the contents of the roasting tin, finishing with the butter. Serve immediately with the freshly ground black pepper and freshly grated Parmigiano Reggiano cheese, to taste.

NOTE: *A cartouche is a piece of baking paper that is used to cover the surface of a dish. It can help to retain moisture, keep the contents submerged, reduce evaporation or prevent a skin forming.*

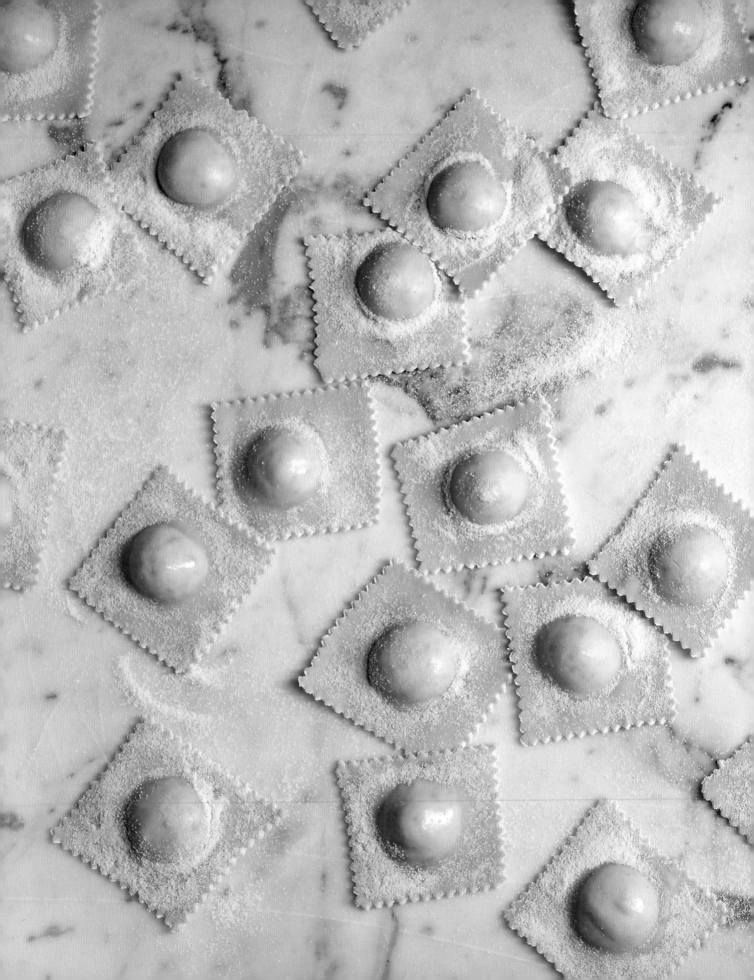

Pasta Ripiena
Filled Pasta

Dove la pasta diventa un'arte
The domain of the artist

For me, filled pasta is more than just a great thing to eat. It's something that I have seen people experience ecstasy over, something that they will travel across the globe to eat. Great filled pasta is about refinement, elegance and balance, it's about changing people's moods, it's about happiness, it's about history and culture, and it's where technique is most important in Italian cooking. It's about food that can and should be art.

Whether it's tortellini, ravioli, mezzelune or any other filled pasta, it's always an exciting process as you transform ingredients into these little works of art. I find that there is usually a great sense of anticipation with filled pasta, more than with other types of pasta, as there is always a degree of uncertainty about what will be contained inside these wonderful little parcels, or how they will actually taste once they are cooked and sauced.

To make superb filled pasta is not easy, but it's definitely worth the effort. Firstly, there is the dough: a science and an art unto itself. Much of the challenge with pasta dough is finding the right thickness for any particular type of filled pasta. Too thick, and the pasta tastes and feels like overcooked dumplings. Too thin, and everything falls apart. Then there is the filling, the quintessential ingredient. It is the most anticipated part of the eating experience and the core of the flavour experience. Then, of course, there is the environment in which you make the pasta. The humidity level, heat and any flow of air in the kitchen can all be very important, more so than most people would imagine. Next you have to store the pasta correctly. This depends on how far in advance you are planning to make the filled pasta, what you are making the pasta with, and the moisture content of the filling, which can be a defining and often frustrating component. Lastly, you have to cook and sauce the filled pasta properly. Each part of the process is important.

The following recipes give detailed steps for each of the filled pastas. When making filled pasta at home, it is fun to get a group of people together to help with the process. It is much less work and everyone has a great time. It's worth the effort!

Ravioli di magro al burro fuso e salvia
Cheese & spinach ravioli with burnt butter & sage

Serves 6 (makes approximately 60 ravioli)

In Italian cooking, vegetables are treated as important and prized ingredients, not simply as nutritious accompaniments or second-class ingredients. They form the essence of great Italian cooking and are treated with a great deal of respect. This dish is a classic example of this. If I was to nominate a dish that most typifies the essence of the Pendolino restaurant experience, this simple dish of spinach and cheese ravioli would probably be it. Many of our regular diners don't even ask for the menu, they simply order the ravioli and that's the end of it. It is the first choice for vegetarians and meat-eaters alike. Done well, this is simply awesome food.

330 g (11½ oz) baby English spinach

260 g (9¼ oz) fresh ricotta cheese

130 g (4½ oz/1¼ cups) freshly grated
   Parmigiano Reggiano cheese,
   plus extra, to serve

100 g (3½ oz/⅔ cup) grated aged
   buffalo mozzarella cheese

⅓ x 59 g (2¼ oz) beaten free-range
   or organic egg

freshly grated nutmeg, to taste

fine sea salt, to taste

freshly ground black pepper, to taste

600 g (1 lb 5 oz) fresh egg pasta
   dough (page 197)

fine semolina, for dusting

200 g (7 oz) salted butter, chopped

12 sage leaves

Prepare the spinach by blanching in boiling water for 2 minutes. Drain and refresh in iced water. Squeeze as much liquid out of the spinach as possible. Process the spinach in a food processor or use a mortar and pestle. Mix with the three cheeses, beaten egg and nutmeg, season with the sea salt and black pepper and set aside.

To make the ravioli, roll the pasta dough into sheets of less than 1 mm (1/32 inch) thickness. Brush one sheet lightly with water and place ½ tablespoon measures of the spinach mixture roughly 5 cm (2 inches) apart. Place another sheet on top, pressing around the mixture to remove air bubbles (this step is essential). Using a circle cutter of approximately 5–5.5 cm (2–2¼ inches) in diameter, cut round ravioli shapes, dust lightly with the semolina and place on tray lined with non-stick baking paper.

Cook the ravioli in abundant salted boiling water and drain. Heat the butter in a saucepan and cook the sage leaves over medium–high heat until golden brown in colour. Serve with the ravioli and extra Parmigiano Reggiano cheese.

Ravioli di mozzarella di bufala e parmigiano reggiano con sugo alla napoletana

Buffalo mozzarella & Parmigiano Reggiano cheese ravioli with neapolitan tomato sauce

Serves 6 (makes approximately 60 ravioli)

250 g (9 oz/2½ cups) freshly grated
  Parmigiano Reggiano cheese,
  plus extra, to serve
250 g (9 oz) baked ricotta
180 g (6¼ oz) aged buffalo
  mozzarella cheese, grated
  (see Note)
600 g (1 lb 5 oz) fresh egg pasta
  dough (page 197)
fine semolina, for dusting
600 ml (21 fl oz) neapolitan tomato
  sauce (page 190)
4 sweet basil leaves

Pulse the three cheeses together in a food processor until well combined. Set aside.

To make the ravioli, roll the pasta dough into sheets of less than 1 mm (¹⁄₃₂ inch) thickness. Brush one sheet lightly with water and place ½ tablespoon measures of the cheese mixture roughly 5 cm (2 inches) apart. Place another sheet on top, pressing around the mixture to remove air bubbles (this step is essential). Using a circle cutter of approximately 5–5.5 cm (2–2¼ inches) in diameter, cut round ravioli shapes, dust lightly with the semolina and place on trays lined with non-stick baking paper.

Heat the neapolitan tomato sauce in a small saucepan. In the meantime, cook the ravioli in abundant salted boiling water until they rise to the surface. Drain the ravioli and add to the sauce. Serve on warm pasta plates. Cut the basil into thin strips (julienne) and distribute over the top of the pasta. Serve with the extra Parmigiano Reggiano cheese.

NOTE: *If you cannot find aged buffalo mozzarella, any aged mozzarella or provola cheese is a suitable replacement; it is simply the cow's milk version.*

Ravioli di patate al coniglio

Potato dough rabbit ravioli with braised rabbit & fava bean sauce

Serves 6 (makes approximately 60 ravioli)

1 whole rabbit (approximately
  1.2 kg/2 lb 10 oz)

fine sea salt, to taste

freshly ground black pepper, to taste

100 ml (3½ fl oz) extra virgin olive oil

1 carrot, roughly sliced

1 celery stalk, roughly sliced

1 brown onion, roughly chopped

1 garlic clove, roughly chopped

160 ml (5¼ fl oz) white wine
  (something sweet, like a Riesling,
  is preferable)

2 litres (70 fl oz/8 cups) chicken broth
  (page 185)

1 bay leaf

3 thyme sprigs

5 black peppercorns

250 g (9 oz) baked ricotta

150 g (5½ oz/1½ cups) freshly grated
  Parmigiano Reggiano cheese, plus
  extra, to serve

600 g (1 lb 5 oz) fresh egg potato
  dough (page 202)

fine semolina, for dusting

100 g (3½ oz) salted butter, chopped

6 fresh broad (fava) beans, podded,
  blanched and peeled (see Note)

Break the rabbit down into the hind legs, the two front legs, the saddle and the rib cage. If you are not sure how to do this, ask your butcher to do it for you. Season with the sea salt and black pepper. Heat the extra virgin olive oil in a large saucepan over medium–high heat and sauté the rabbit until golden in colour. Remove and set aside. Add the vegetables to the pan and cook until brown. Return the rabbit to the pan and deglaze with the white wine. Once the wine has evaporated, add the chicken broth, herbs and peppercorns. Bring to the boil and simmer for approximately 2 hours, or until the meat is falling off the bones. Strain, reserving the liquid. Retain the meat but discard the vegetables, herbs and peppercorns. Cool slightly, then pick the meat from the bones and refrigerate until chilled.

For the sauce, reduce the reserved braising liquid to about 375 ml (13 fl oz/1½ cups) until it is a sauce consistency, skimming the oil and residue regularly. Set aside.

In a food processor, pulse the meat with the baked ricotta cheese and Parmigiano Reggiano cheese until combined. Try not to make a purée as you want some of the texture of the meat to remain. Season with the sea salt and black pepper.

To make the ravioli, roll the pasta dough into sheets of less than 1 mm (1/32 inch) thickness. Brush one sheet lightly with water and place ½ tablespoon measures of the rabbit mixture roughly 5 cm (2 inches) apart. Place another sheet on top, pressing around the mixture to remove air bubbles (this step is essential). Using a circle cutter of approximately 5–5.5cm (2–2¼ inches), cut a round ravioli shape, dust lightly with the semolina and place on trays lined with non-stick baking paper.

In a small frying pan, melt the butter over medium–high heat until it is a dark golden brown colour. Set aside.

Cook the ravioli in abundant salted boiling water, adding the broad beans for the final 15 seconds (be careful not to overcook them). Drain and serve with the rabbit sauce, browned butter, broad beans and extra Parmigiano Reggiano cheese.

NOTE: *To peel fresh broad beans, first blanch them in boiling water for 30 seconds. Drain and chill in iced water, then strain and squeeze the beans out of their skins.*

Tortellini di carne alla bolognese con ragù

Meat tortellini with classic bolognaise sauce

Serves 6 (makes approximately 60 tortellini)

60 g (2¼ oz) butter

2 tablespoons extra virgin olive oil

180 g (6¼ oz) minced (ground) veal

180 g (6¼ oz) minced (ground) pork

180 g (6¼ oz) cooked chicken flesh
(from chicken broth recipe on
page 185), minced (ground)

fine sea salt, to taste

freshly ground black pepper, to taste

180 g (6¼ oz) minced (ground)
prosciutto

180 g (6¼ oz) minced (ground)
mortadella

100 ml (3½ fl oz) dry white wine

freshly grated nutmeg, to taste

150 g (5½ oz/1½ cups) freshly grated
Parmigiano Reggiano cheese,
plus extra, to serve (optional)

1 x 59 g (2¼ oz) free-range
or organic egg

400 g (14 oz) fresh egg pasta dough
(page 197)

fine semolina, for dusting

500 g (1 lb 2 oz) bolognaise sauce
(page 194)

In a large saucepan, melt the butter with the extra virgin olive oil over medium–high heat. Add the minced veal, pork and chicken flesh and sauté until brown. Season with the sea salt and black pepper. After about 10 minutes the meat will start to release its juices. At this point, add the prosciutto and mortadella and cook for a further 10 minutes or until the juices evaporate. Add the white wine to deglaze the pan and cook for a further 10 minutes or until the wine has completely evaporated. Set aside and allow to cool. When cooled, add the nutmeg, Parmigiano Reggiano cheese and egg, and season. Process the mixture in a food processor until all the ingredients are combined. You will only need half of the filling, so freeze the remainder for next time.

To make the tortellini, roll the pasta dough into sheets of less than 1 mm (1/32 inch) thickness. Cut the pasta into squares of approximately 4.5 x 4.5 cm (1¾ x 1¾ inches). The size of the pasta square is a personal preference and can vary a great deal in Bologna and throughout Italy. Place ½ teaspoon measures of the filling in the centre of each of the pasta squares and fold the square into a triangle, making sure to press out any air. Press down on the edges so that the pasta completely seals the filling. This is quite a wet dough and pressing alone should bind the two sheets of pasta together. If it is a hot day and the pasta is drying quickly, use a pastry brush and brush a little water onto the edges of the squares before folding. This will help them stick together. Quickly fold down the top of the triangle and roll the other two edges of the triangle together (I use my little finger as a mould for this) to form what look like little hats. Dust lightly with the semolina and place on trays lined with non-stick baking paper until ready to use. They should be made as close to the eating time as possible, although they can be stored in an airtight container and frozen for later use.

Heat the bolognaise sauce in a saucepan. Meanwhile, bring abundant salted water to the boil and cook the tortellini for 10 minutes or until they rise to the surface. Strain the tortellini, mix with the heated bolognaise sauce and serve with the extra Parmigiano Reggiano cheese, if desired.

Ravioli di piselli e ricotta con fonduta di gorgonzola e burro fuso

Sweet pea ravioli with gorgonzola cream & burnt butter

Serves 6 (makes approximately 60 ravioli)

The Pendolino and La Rosa Bar and Pizza restaurants are set in one of Sydney's most beautiful buildings, the Strand Arcade. The only remaining Victorian-era arcade in Sydney, it houses an eclectic and boutique mix of artisan jewellers, leather craftsmen and accomplished Australian fashion designers. We have initiated a range of special events in the restaurants that have been enormously popular, including a 'meet the designer' lunch. This is a pasta dish that I created for one of these events. It was a knockout hit and we periodically feature it as one of our seasonal specials.

135 ml (4½ fl oz) vegetable broth (page 187)

2 tablespoons extra virgin olive oil

35 g (1¼ oz) salted butter, chopped, plus extra 100 g (3½ oz) for burnt butter

½ small onion, finely diced

3 thyme sprigs, picked

1 garlic clove, finely diced

750 g (1 lb 10 oz) peas in the pod, yielding about 260 g (9¼ oz) fresh peas

165 g (5¾ oz/⅔ cup) fresh ricotta cheese

90 g (3¼ oz/1 cup) freshly grated Parmigiano Reggiano cheese, plus extra, to serve

fine sea salt, to taste

freshly ground black pepper, to taste

600 g (1 lb 5 oz) fresh egg pasta dough (page 197)

fine semolina, for dusting

300 ml (10½ fl oz) cream

150 g (5½ oz) gorgonzola cheese, chopped

Heat the vegetable broth in a saucepan, bring to the boil, then turn off the heat. Heat the extra virgin olive oil and butter in a separate large saucepan over low–medium heat and cook the onion, thyme and garlic until soft. Add the peas and vegetable broth. Increase the heat to high and bring to the boil quickly. Take off the heat and transfer the mixture to a food processor. Pulse into a rough purée (you still want some texture from the peas). Allow to cool. Mix with the ricotta cheese and 65 g (2¼ oz) of the Parmigiano Reggiano cheese and season with the sea salt and black pepper, to taste.

To make the ravioli, roll the pasta dough into sheets of less than 1 mm (1/32 inch) thickness. Brush one sheet lightly with water and place ½ tablespoon measures of the pea mixture roughly 5 cm (2 inches) apart. Place another sheet on top, pressing around the mixture to remove air bubbles (this step is essential). With a round roller or jagged-edged cutter, cut out square ravioli (or whichever shape you desire), dust lightly with the semolina and place on trays lined with non-stick baking paper.

To make the sauce, pour the cream into a small saucepan and reduce by a third over medium heat. Add the gorgonzola cheese and the remaining Parmigiano Reggiano cheese and stir occasionally until the cheeses melt. Make this sauce as close to serving as possible.

For the burnt butter, simply heat the extra butter in a saucepan over medium–high heat until it starts to go dark golden.

To serve, cook the ravioli in abundant salted boiling water until they rise to the surface. Drain and serve with the gorgonzola cream, burnt butter and extra Parmigiano Reggiano cheese.

Ravioli neri ripieni di capesanti con salsetta di crostacei

Black scallop ravioli with crustacean reduction sauce

Serves 6 (makes approximately 60 ravioli)

This dish is another perennial classic at Pendolino. Every time we take it off the menu, we spend the next six months listening to the laments of our customers who desperately want it back. My response is usually the same: 'Yes, it is a lovely dish, but we have to change something on the menu!' It is a great dish. We use a scallop product that has international Marine Stewardship Council (MSC) certification. This means that the product is sustainably caught, which is a great thing for the world's oceans. The MSC is an invaluable global organisation and we try to support them as much as we can.

100 ml (3½ fl oz) extra virgin olive oil, plus extra for drizzling

400 g (14 oz) scallop meat

2 garlic cloves, finely chopped

100 ml (3½ fl oz) white wine

50 g (1¾ oz) English spinach, steamed, drained and chopped (make sure excess moisture has been squeezed out)

400 g (14 oz/1⅔ cups) fresh ricotta cheese

fine sea salt, to taste

freshly ground black pepper, to taste

600 g (1 lb 5 oz) squid/cuttlefish ink fresh egg pasta dough (page 209)

fine semolina, for dusting

500 ml (17 fl oz/2 cups) crustacean broth (page 189)

100 ml (3½ fl oz) fish broth (page 189)

2½ tablespoons good-quality tomato passata (puréed tomatoes)

1 tablespoon thick (double/heavy) cream

120 g (4¼ oz) salted butter, cold, chopped

baby flat-leaf (Italian) parsley leaves, to serve

For the filling, heat the extra virgin olive oil in frying pan over medium–high heat and add the scallops and garlic. When the scallops are just cooked, deglaze the pan with the white wine. Strain the mixture and cool. Add the spinach to the mixture and pulse in a food processor until roughly chopped. Stir through the ricotta cheese, season to taste with the sea salt and black pepper, and refrigerate.

To make the ravioli, roll the pasta dough into sheets of less than 1 mm (1/32 inch) thickness. Brush one sheet lightly with water and place ½ tablespoon measures of the mixture roughly 5 cm (2 inches) apart. Place another sheet on top, pressing around the mixture to remove air bubbles (this step is essential). With a round or jagged-edged cutter, cut out square ravioli (or whichever shape you desire), dust lightly with the semolina and place on trays lined with non-stick baking paper.

For the sauce, place the crustacean broth in a saucepan and reduce to 400 ml (14 fl oz). Add the fish broth and tomato passata, bring to the boil, then whisk in the cream. Take off the heat and whisk in the butter to slightly thicken the sauce.

Cook the ravioli in abundant salted boiling water until they rise to the surface. Serve with the crustacean sauce, a drizzle of extra virgin olive oil and the baby parsley leaves.

Mezzelune di maiale

Pork belly ravioli with pork belly, pork cheek & pork sauce

Serves 6 (makes approximately 90 ravioli)

300 g (10½ oz) pork belly, cut into
2.5 cm (1 inch) pieces

600 g (1 lb 5 oz) denuded pork cheek
(see Note)

3 garlic cloves

3 thyme sprigs

1 rosemary sprig

6 black peppercorns

1.5 litres (52 fl oz/6 cups) chicken
broth (page 185)

fine sea salt, to taste

freshly ground black pepper, to taste

2 teaspoons fennel seeds

500 ml (17 fl oz/2 cups) beef broth
(page 187)

25 g (1 oz) minced (ground)
prosciutto

70 g (2½ oz/⅔ cup) freshly grated
Parmigiano Reggiano cheese,
plus extra, to serve

275 g (9¾ oz) fresh ricotta cheese

600 g (1 lb 5 oz) fresh egg pasta
dough (page 197)

fine semolina, for dusting

Preheat the oven to 180°C (350°F/Gas 4).

Place the pork belly, pork cheek, garlic, thyme, rosemary, peppercorns, chicken broth, sea salt and black pepper in a small roasting tray, making sure the pork is covered with the broth. Cover tightly with foil and bake for 2 hours or until the meat is tender. Remove the meat and set aside covered with a tea towel (dish towel) moistened with some of the cooking liquor. When it has cooled a little, place in the refrigerator. Just before doing this, strain the braising liquid and place in a medium-sized saucepan with the fennel seeds and beef broth. Reduce slowly to 375 ml (13 fl oz/1½ cups), skimming oil and residue regularly. This will take approximately 1.5–2 hours. Set aside.

To make the filling, mince the refrigerated pork belly. Shred the cheeks and set aside to add to the sauce later. Mix the minced pork belly in a large bowl with the prosciutto, Parmigiano Reggiano cheese, ricotta cheese and seasoning.

To make the mezzelune, roll the sheets of egg pasta dough to less than 1 mm (1/32 inch) in thickness and cut into round discs roughly 6 cm (2½ inches) in diameter with a pastry cutter. Place a teaspoon of filling on one side of each of the discs and fold the other side to form half-moon ravioli, making sure to remove as much air as possible. Press the edges down to seal with your fingers. Tidy the edges up by trimming with a slightly smaller pastry cutter. Dust with the semolina and place on trays lined with non-stick baking paper.

Reheat the shredded pork cheek in the reduced sauce. Cook the ravioli in abundant salted boiling water. Drain and serve with the heated pork sauce and extra Parmigiano Reggiano cheese.

NOTE: *You may need to order the pork cheek in advance from a specialist butcher. Ask the butcher to denude the pork cheek for you (i.e. trim it completely of fat).*

Tortelli di zucca con amaretti e pistacchi

Pumpkin tortelli with pistachio nuts, amaretti biscuits, Parmigiano Reggiano & burnt butter

Serves 6 (makes approximately 36 tortelli)

300 g (10½ oz) butternut pumpkin (squash)

1 garlic clove, unpeeled

150 g (5½ oz) fresh ricotta cheese

25 g (1 oz) mustard fruits, deseeded (see Note)

40 g (1½ oz) freshly grated Parmigiano Reggiano cheese, plus extra, to serve

fine sea salt, to taste

freshly ground black pepper, to taste

600 g (1 lb 5 oz) fresh egg pasta dough (page 197)

fine semolina, for dusting

150 g (5½ oz) salted butter, chopped

50 pistachio nuts, roasted and roughly crushed

2 amaretti biscuits, crushed to medium–fine breadcrumb size (these are very sweet biscuits and should be used according to personal taste)

NOTE: *This is an Italian product in which fruit is preserved in a heavy syrup that is flavoured with mustard.*

Preheat the oven to 130°C (250°F/Gas 1).

Peel, deseed and dice the pumpkin into approximately 3 cm (1¼ inch) pieces. Place on a baking tray with the garlic and cover tightly with foil. Roast the pumpkin for 45 minutes and then uncovered for another 30–45 minutes, or until tender. Strain the liquid away and refrigerate until cool.

Remove the pumpkin from the refrigerator and squeeze out any excess liquid. Put the pumpkin in a food processor with the peeled roasted garlic, ricotta cheese, mustard fruits, Parmigiano Reggiano cheese, sea salt and black pepper and pulse to combine.

Roll the pasta dough sheets to less than 1 mm (1/32 inch) thickness. Cut the pasta into squares that are approximately 9 x 9 cm (3½ x 3½ inches) in size. Place a heaped teaspoon of the pumpkin mixture in the centre of each of the pasta squares and then fold into a triangle, making sure to press out any air. Press down on the edges so that the pasta completely seals the filling. This is quite a wet dough so pressing alone should bind the two sheets of pasta together. If it is a hot day and the pasta is drying quickly, use a pastry brush and brush a little water onto the edges of the squares before folding. This will help them stick together. Quickly fold down the tip of the top of the triangle and roll the other two edges of the triangle together (I use my little finger as a mould for this) to form little hats. Dust with the fine semolina and place on trays lined with non-stick baking paper until ready to use. They should be made as close to serving time as possible, although they can be stored in an airtight container and frozen for later use.

Heat the butter in a large saucepan over medium–high heat until it becomes golden brown in colour. Set aside.

To serve, simply cook the tortelli in abundant salted boiling water until they rise to the surface. Drain and serve with the extra Parmigiano Reggiano cheese and the burnt butter sauce. Finish with a sprinkling of the crushed pistachio nuts and amaretti biscuits.

Ravioli di agnello e animelle con asparagi bianchi e verdi

Lamb & sweetbread ravioli with braised lamb & white & green asparagus sauce

Serves 6 (makes approximately 90 ravioli)

1 kg (2 lb 4 oz) lamb shanks

fine sea salt, to taste

freshly ground black pepper, to taste

plain (all-purpose) flour, for dusting

25 g (1 oz) butter, plus 20 g (¾ oz)
   for frying sweetbreads

1 tablespoon extra virgin olive
   oil, plus 1 tablespoon for frying
   sweetbreads

300 g (10½ oz) lamb sweetbreads

1 brown onion, roughly chopped

1 celery stalk, roughly chopped

1 carrot, roughly chopped

1 bay leaf

1 teaspoon lemon juice

1 teaspoon white wine vinegar

1 garlic clove, peeled

100 ml (3½ fl oz) red wine

1 thyme sprig

1 rosemary sprig

2.3 litres (80½ fl oz) chicken broth
   (page 185)

100 g (3½ oz/1 cup) freshly grated
   Parmigiano Reggiano cheese

600 g (1 lb 5 oz) fresh egg pasta
   dough (page 197)

fine semolina, for dusting

3 green asparagus spears, sliced
   2 mm (1⁄16 inch) thin on an angle

3 white asparagus spears, sliced
   2 mm (1⁄16 inch) thin on an angle

Season the lamb shanks with the sea salt and black pepper and dust with flour. Shake off excess flour and pan-fry in the butter and extra virgin olive oil over medium heat until brown. Set aside.

In a small saucepan, put the sweetbreads, half the onion, half the celery and half the carrot, then add the bay leaf, lemon juice, vinegar and garlic. Cover with water and season. Bring to the boil, turn down to a simmer and cook for 2 minutes more. Take off the heat and run the sweetbreads under cold water until cool. Discard the cooking liquid and vegetables.

Peel the skin and fat off the sweetbreads, dice and then pan-fry half of them over medium–high heat in 10 g (¼ oz) of the butter and ½ tablespoon of the extra virgin olive oil until fully cooked. Set aside and cool.

To make the filling, add the remaining diced vegetables to the pan in which you sealed the shanks, place over medium heat and sauté till browned. Add the red wine and reduce by half, then add the shanks, thyme and rosemary and cover with the chicken broth. Bring to the boil and reduce the heat to a simmer and cook for approximately 2–2½ hours, or until the meat falls off the bone. Remove the meat from the bones, discarding the gristle and half of the fat.   »

Roughly chop the meat and fat and pulse in a food processor with the cooked sweetbreads until it is almost a paste, then stir through the Parmigiano Reggiano cheese.

Reduce the shank cooking liquid over medium heat to a sauce consistency, skimming off any fat until reduced to 375 ml (13 fl oz/1½ cups). Strain the sauce and set aside.

To make the ravioli, roll the pasta dough to approximately 1 mm (⅟₃₂ inch) thickness. Cut round shapes about 6 cm (2½ inches) in diameter using a pastry cutter. Place 1 teaspoon of the meat mixture onto each circle and fold the pasta over to form a *mezzaluna* (half-moon). Press down the edges to seal. Use a small cutter to neaten the edges if desired. Dust lightly with the semolina and place on trays lined with non-stick baking paper. Pan-fry the remaining sweetbreads over medium–high heat in the remaining 10 g (¼ oz) butter and ½ tablespoon extra virgin olive oil until crisp and golden.

Cook the ravioli and asparagus slices in abundant salted boiling water until they rise to the surface. Serve with the crispy sweetbreads and sauce.

Agnolotti di gamberi con salsetta di pomodoro e olive

Prawn agnolotti with tomato, olive & prawn sauce

Serves 6 (makes approximately 60 ravioli)

⅓ cup extra virgin olive oil

300 g (10½ oz) prawn meat

1½ garlic cloves, chopped

80 ml (2½ fl oz/⅓ cup) white wine

40 g (1½ oz) English spinach, steamed, drained and chopped (make sure excess moisture has been squeezed out)

300 g (10½ oz) fresh ricotta cheese

fine sea salt, to taste

freshly ground black pepper, to taste

600 g (1 lb 5 oz) fresh egg pasta dough (page 197)

fine semolina, for dusting

flat-leaf (Italian) parsley, chopped, to serve

SAUCE

⅓ cup extra virgin olive oil

250 g (9 oz) prawn meat, minced

250 g (9 oz) onions, finely diced

25 g (1 oz) garlic, finely diced

2½ tablespoons white wine

350 ml (12 fl oz) good-quality tomato passata (puréed tomatoes)

25 g (1 oz) dried pitted black olives, thinly sliced

1 teaspoon garum (fermented fish sauce)

Heat the extra virgin olive oil in a saucepan over medium–high heat and add the prawn meat and garlic. Cook until the prawn meat is just cooked and deglaze with the white wine. Reduce the wine and oil by a third. Strain the mixture and cool, then add the spinach. Pulse the prawn and spinach mixture in a food processor until roughly chopped. Stir through the ricotta cheese and season with the sea salt and black pepper, then refrigerate.

To make the ravioli, roll the pasta dough into sheets of less than 1 mm (1/32 inch) thickness. Brush one sheet lightly with water and place ½ tablespoon measures of the mixture roughly 5 cm (2 inches) apart. Place another sheet on top, pressing around the mixture to remove air bubbles (this step is essential). With a jagged-edged cutter, cut out square ravioli (or whatever shape you desire), dust lightly with the semolina and place on trays lined with non-stick baking paper.

To make the sauce, heat the extra virgin olive oil in a large saucepan over medium–high heat and sauté the prawn meat, onion and garlic until the onion and garlic are translucent. Deglaze with the white wine and reduce by half. Add the tomato passata, olives and garum and gently cook for 20 minutes. Set aside.

To serve, simply cook the ravioli in abundant salted boiling water until they rise to the surface. Heat the sauce and serve on a plate, placing the ravioli on top of a pool of sauce.

Pasta al Forno

Baked Pasta

Dal conte al contadino
From count to country folk

Baked pasta almost perfectly typifies Italian cuisine. On the one hand, it is something that has largely evolved out of sheer need. In feudal times, *contadini* (field workers or farmers) needed a transportable meal to eat during the day. Baked pasta was a one-pot nutritious meal without the pot. *Vincisgrassi* from Le Marche is a great example of this. The ingredients of the dish have varied since the 1700s, depending on the season and the availability of produce. Apart from the core ingredients of chicken livers and mushrooms, the other components are perfectly substitutable, as long as they taste good and can be successfully baked into the dish.

On the other hand, baked pasta is often at the centre of Italy's greatest celebrations. Elaborate versions were developed and eaten in the royal courts and by the gentry for special occasions. It has also been centre stage in Italian culture's most important ritualistic and celebratory events. Lasagne is eaten all over Italy for events such as Christmas, and the Neapolitan *lasagne di carnevale* is a great example of how culture, cuisine and religion perfectly combine. This dish, packed with a plethora of meats, ritualistically signifies the last indulgence before Lenten fasting.

I particularly enjoy cooking baked pasta when entertaining large groups at home as it is a very easy way to impress a lot of people and can be prepared in advance. This chapter contains a range of baked pasta dishes that are sure to please different palates and tastes, from wonderful meat-based dishes, such as the aforementioned *vincisgrassi* and my personal favourite *lasagne millefoglie*, through to a range of delicious vegetable pasta bakes. I have also included *gnocchi alla romana* with beautiful red wine-braised lamb where the baked pasta works perfectly as an accompaniment for a predominantely protein-based dish. *Buon appetito!*

Gnocchi alla sorrentina al forno

Baked gnocchi with tomato & basil sauce & buffalo mozzarella cheese

Serves 6

350 ml (12 fl oz) neapolitan tomato
    sauce (page 190)
6 sweet basil leaves
fine sea salt, to taste
600 g (1 lb 5 oz) potato gnocchi
    (page 212)
200 g (7 oz) fresh buffalo mozzarella
    cheese, processed in a food
    processor to breadcrumb size
100 g (3½ oz/1 cup) freshly grated
    Parmigiano Reggiano cheese

Preheat the oven to 180°C (350°F/Gas 4). Heat the sauce with the basil leaves in a saucepan and season with the sea salt and black pepper, to taste. In abundant salted boiling water, cook the gnocchi until they rise to the surface. Strain the gnocchi, mix with the sauce and place in a large, greased baking dish, or individual baking dishes, and top with the buffalo mozzarella and Parmigiano Reggiano cheese. Bake for approximately 20 minutes or until the cheese is golden brown.

Vincisgrassi
Abruzzese chicken liver &
mushroom lasagne with truffle

Serves 6

This classic Abruzzese dish has developed quite a cult following at Caffè Pendolino. It has become virtually impossible to take off the menu, which is wonderful for a dish made with offal. As with all baked pasta dishes, it can be made with dried pasta sheets, but it is much better if fresh pasta is used. The addition of fresh truffles can take this dish from great to extraordinary, and if you are ever in Italy during mushroom season and have the chance to substitute the portobello mushrooms for fresh porcini, the dish will become something different again, adding a unique meatiness and sublime flavour. Fresh porcini are the king of fresh mushrooms in my book.

100 ml (3½ fl oz) extra virgin olive oil

400 g (14 oz) chicken livers,
  cleaned and finely chopped

fine sea salt, to taste

freshly ground black pepper, to taste

50 g (1¾ oz) butter

1 onion, finely diced

1 carrot, finely diced

½ celery stalk, finely diced

1 garlic clove, finely diced

1 rosemary sprig, picked

1 teaspoon dried oregano

600 g (1 lb 5 oz) portobello
  mushrooms, sliced

400 ml (14 fl oz) red wine

400 ml (14 fl oz) good-quality tomato
  passata (puréed tomatoes)

25 g (1 oz) fresh truffle, thinly sliced
  (see Note)

750 ml (26 fl oz/3 cups) béchamel
  sauce (page 193)

300 g (10½ oz) fresh egg pasta dough
  (page 197), rolled into pasta sheets
  no thicker than 1 mm (¹⁄₃₂ inch)

150 g (5½ oz/1½ cups) freshly grated
  Parmigiano Reggiano cheese

Preheat the oven to 180°C (350°F/Gas 4). In a large frying pan, heat half of the extra virgin olive oil over high heat and fry the chicken livers until sealed. Remove from the pan, season with the sea salt and black pepper, to taste, and set aside.

Heat the butter and remaining extra virgin olive oil in a large saucepan over medium heat. Sauté the vegetables, garlic and herbs until the onion and garlic become translucent. Add the mushrooms and sauté until all the liquid has evaporated. Add the red wine and reduce by half. Add the tomato passata and simmer for 10 minutes. Add the sealed chicken livers and truffle oil (if not using fresh truffle). Check seasoning and set aside.

To make the lasagne, grease a 24 x 20 x 5 cm (9½ x 8 x 2 inch) baking dish. Reserve 150 ml (5 fl oz) of the béchamel for the topping. Spread the base with a little of the chicken liver ragù. Place some of the pasta sheets on the bottom of the dish, followed by a quarter of the chicken liver ragù and a quarter of the remaining béchamel. Place some very thin slices of truffle (if not using truffle oil) on top of the béchamel sauce. Repeat three times. Top the lasagne with the reserved béchamel, Parmigiano Reggiano cheese and more truffle. Bake for approximately 20–30 minutes or until the cheese has turned golden brown. Serve hot or reheat later.

NOTE: *As an alternative to fresh truffle, use 2 teaspoons white truffle oil, plus extra for serving.*

Gnocchi alla romana con brasato di agnello all'aglianico e scorzanera

Roman baked gnocchi with Aglianico red wine-braised lamb neck & black salsify

Serves 6

Outside of Rome, Roman gnocchi can cause a great deal of confusion. To most people, gnocchi means only one thing: fresh little pasta dumplings made from boiled potato, egg and flour. The term 'gnocchi', however, can be used to describe various other pasta incarnations, such as Sardinian gnocchi, a dried pasta that has a similar shape to classic gnocchi but that contains no potato. There are also dishes such as gnocchi di susine *(page 165), a dessert gnocchi, which is quite different again.*

In reality, gnocchi alla romana *is more akin to what we know as polenta. This makes sense as polenta was made with wheat flour before corn arrived from the Americas. This dish is extremely versatile and can be eaten alone with plenty of Parmigiano Reggiano cheese melted on top, or as an accompaniment. It is one of my favourite accompaniments for meat dishes, and I have rarely left it off a menu as it works so well with a range of meat dishes, particularly braises. This lamb braised in Aglianico red wine is stunning with the gnocchi.*

SEMOLINA GNOCCHI

560 ml (19¼ fl oz/2¼ cups)
  full-cream (whole) milk
75 g (2½ oz) salted butter, chopped
fine sea salt, to taste
150 g (5½ oz) fine semolina
2 free-range or organic egg yolks
75 g (2½ oz/¾ cup) freshly grated
  Parmigiano Reggiano cheese,
  plus extra for topping

CARAMELISED SALSIFY

about 400 g (14 oz) salsify
  (scorzanera)
2½ tablespoons extra virgin olive oil
50 g (1¾ oz) butter
fine sea salt, to taste
freshly ground black pepper, to taste

To make the semolina gnocchi, bring the milk to the boil in a large heavy-based saucepan, then add the butter and a pinch of the sea salt. Pour in the semolina, stirring constantly, and cook over low heat for 15 minutes. Leave to cool slightly and then stir through the egg yolks and Parmigiano Reggiano cheese.

Pour the mixture into a buttered baking tin so it is about 3 cm (1¼ inches) thick. Cool to room temperature and refrigerate until firm. Cut into desired shapes, such as 5 cm (2 inch) rounds or squares, and place in a large, greased, ovenproof baking dish and top with the extra Parmigiano Reggiano cheese. Set aside.

To make the caramelised salsify, wash, peel and re-wash the salsify, then cut it into 10 cm (4 inch) lengths. Blanch the salsify in salted boiling water until half cooked. Remove from the water, refresh in iced water and place in a bowl with the extra virgin olive oil, butter, sea salt and black pepper. Place the dressed salsify into a roasting tin and set aside. »

BRAISED LAMB

1.5 kg (3 lb 5 oz) boneless lamb neck pieces

fine sea salt, to taste

freshly ground black pepper, to taste

100 ml (3½ fl oz) extra virgin olive oil

1 carrot, cut into 1 cm (½ inch) dice

1 celery stalk, cut into 1 cm (½ inch) dice

1 onion, cut into 1 cm (½ inch) dice

1 tablespoon double-strength tomato paste (concentrated purée)

600 ml (21 fl oz) Aglianico red wine or similar (Sangiovese, Nebbiolo or Cabernet Sauvignon are good substitutes)

4 garlic cloves

10 g (¼ oz) dried porcini mushrooms, twice-washed in hot water and strained

500 ml (17 fl oz/2 cups) chicken broth (page 185) or beef broth (page 187)

1 thyme sprig

1 rosemary sprig

1 bay leaf

a few flat-leaf (Italian) parsley sprigs

To make the braised lamb, trim the lamb pieces, keeping some fat on. Season with the sea salt and black pepper. In a large saucepan, heat the extra virgin olive oil over medium heat and sear both sides of the lamb. Remove from the saucepan and set aside. Brown the vegetables in the same saucepan. Add the tomato paste and deglaze the pan with the red wine and reduce until it is completely evaporated. Return the lamb to the pan and add the remaining ingredients. Bring to the boil and turn down to a simmer for 1½–2 hours, or until the meat starts falling apart. Make sure to keep the meat submerged during cooking. Placing a baking paper cartouche can assist with this (page 78). Take the meat from the pan and continue to cook to reduce the sauce until it is the desired consistency and flavour. Be careful not to over-reduce the sauce as it will become overpowering. Return the meat to the sauce, gently reheat and check seasoning.

Meanwhile, preheat the oven to 180°C (350°F/Gas 4). Bake both the salsify and semolina gnocchi for 20 minutes or until golden brown. They may have slightly different cooking times. Serve the lamb with the semolina gnocchi and caramelised salsify.

Pizzoccheri al forno

Baked buckwheat noodles with cabbage & fontina

Serves 6

3 potatoes, unpeeled

100 ml (3½ fl oz) extra virgin olive oil

2 leeks, cut into 1 cm (½ inch) dice

6 garlic cloves

150 g (5½ oz) savoy cabbage,
chopped into 3 cm (1¼ inch)
squares

6 sage leaves

fine sea salt, to taste

freshly ground black pepper, to taste

450 g (1 lb) buckwheat fresh egg
pasta (page 203)

150 g (5½ oz) fontina cheese,
chopped

250 g (9 oz/2½ cups) freshly grated
Parmigiano Reggiano cheese,
plus extra, to serve (optional)

Preheat the oven to 180°C (350°F/Gas 4). Boil the potatoes until almost cooked. Drain, allow to cool, then slice (unpeeled) carefully with a serrated knife. Set aside.

Heat the extra virgin olive oil in a large saucepan and sauté the leeks, garlic, cabbage and sage until softened. Season with the sea salt and black pepper and set aside.

Cook the pasta in abundant salted boiling water until slightly under *al dente*. Drain and mix with the sautéed cabbage mixture.

To assemble the pasta bake, grease a 24 x 20 x 5 cm (9½ x 8 x 2 inch) ovenproof dish. Layer the ingredients much like making a lasagne. Spread half of the pasta and cabbage mixture on the bottom of the dish. Layer half of the potato, then place the remaining pasta mixture on top. Top with the remaining potato, fontina cheese and Parmigiano Reggiano cheese.

Bake for approximately 25 minutes or until the cheese is golden brown in colour. Serve with additional Parmigiano Reggiano cheese, if desired.

Pasta e patate al forno con scamorza
Baked penne with potatoes & scamorza cheese
Serves 6

50 g (1¾ oz) butter

2½ tablespoons extra virgin olive oil

1 medium onion, diced

100 g (3½ oz) sliced pancetta,
  chopped

2 sage leaves

2 oregano sprigs

500 ml (17 fl oz/2 cups) good-quality
  tomato passata (puréed tomatoes)

400 g (14 oz) good-quality dried
  penne pasta

300 g (10½ oz) potatoes, diced into
  1 cm (½ inch) cubes, kept in
  chilled water

350 g (12 oz) scamorza cheese,
  thinly sliced

200 g (7 oz) fresh ricotta cheese

fine sea salt, to taste

freshly grated black pepper, to taste

250 g (9 oz/2½ cups) freshly grated
  Parmigiano Reggiano cheese

Preheat the oven to 180°C (350°F/Gas 4). Heat the butter and extra virgin olive oil in a small saucepan over medium heat and sauté the onion, pancetta, sage and oregano until the onion is fully cooked and soft. Add the tomato passata and cook for a further 15 minutes. Set aside. Cook the pasta in abundant salted boiling water until just under *al dente*. Drain and mix the pasta with the tomato sauce. Set aside. Place the potatoes in a saucepan, cover with water and boil until just cooked.

To assemble the pasta bake, grease a 24 x 20 x 5 cm (9½ x 8 x 2 inch) ovenproof dish. Layer the ingredients much like making lasagne. Spread half of the pasta and tomato mix on the bottom. Layer half of the scamorza cheese and then the ricotta, seasoning as you go with the sea salt and black pepper. Place the remaining pasta mixture in the dish and top with the potatoes and then the remaining scamorza cheese. Finish with the freshly grated Parmigiano Reggiano cheese. Bake for 15–20 minutes or until the cheese is golden brown.

Lasagne millefoglie
Thousand-layer lasagne

Serves 6

750 ml (26 fl oz/3 cups) béchamel
   sauce (page 193)
300 g (10½ oz) fresh egg pasta dough
   (page 197), rolled into sheets no
   thicker than 1 mm (1/32 inch)
650 g (1 lb 7 oz) bolognaise sauce
   (page 194)
300 g (10½ oz/3 cups) freshly grated
   Parmigiano Reggiano cheese
freshly grated nutmeg, to taste

Preheat the oven to 180°C (350°F/Gas 4).

To make the lasagne, grease a 24 x 20 x 5 cm (9½ x 8 x 2 inch) ovenproof baking dish. Reserve 150 ml (5 fl oz) of the béchamel for the topping. Spread the base of the baking dish with some of the béchamel. Place some of the pasta sheets on the bottom of the dish, followed by a quarter of the bolognaise sauce and a quarter of the remaining béchamel sauce. Sprinkle some Parmigiano Reggiano cheese over the béchamel. Repeat three times. Spread the reserved béchamel sauce and cover with the remaining Parmigiano Reggiano cheese and nutmeg, to taste. Bake for approximately 50–60 minutes or until the cheese has turned golden brown.

Rotolo di cavolfiore e ricotta
Pasta roll filled with fried cauliflower & ricotta

Serves 6

2½ tablespoons extra virgin olive oil

500 g (1 lb 2 oz) cauliflower, cut into very small florets and blanched

1 garlic clove, finely diced

250 g (9 oz) fresh egg pasta dough (page 197), divided into two balls and set aside to rest

400 g (14 oz/1⅔ cup) fresh ricotta cheese

30 g (1 oz) flat-leaf (Italian) parsley leaves, roughly chopped

100 g (3½ oz/1 cup) coarsely grated gruyère cheese

50 g (1¾ oz) salted butter, chopped

40 g (1½ oz/⅓ cup) fresly grated Parmigiano Reggiano cheese, plus extra, to serve

sliced fresh truffle, to taste (optional)

Heat the extra virgin olive oil in a large frying pan over medium heat and sauté the cauliflower and garlic until lightly golden. Set aside to cool.

To make the pasta roll, roll the balls of pasta dough to 1 mm (1/32 inch) thick (see Note). This should yield two sheets of approximately 75 x 14 cm (29 x 5½ inches). Cut into 3 crossways. Lay 3 of these sheets onto muslin (cheesecloth), overlapping by 1 cm (½ inch) to form a sheet of pasta about 40 x 25 cm (16 x 10 inches). Brush the joins lightly with water to seal. Repeat with the other 3 sheets on top. Crumble the ricotta evenly on the sheets followed by the parsley leaves, gruyère cheese and the cauliflower mix, leaving a 5 cm (2 inch) gap at the end and a 3 cm (1¼ inch) gap at the sides.

Roll the pasta roll from the longer side, being sure to roll tightly. Seal the end with a little water and fold in the sides. Wrap tightly in the muslin and tie the ends with a piece of string. Place the pasta roll in a fish boiler of boiling water (if this is unavailable, simply use a large stockpot with water and bring to the boil). Cook for approximately 30 minutes. You may need to weigh it down with a rack and turn it halfway through cooking. Remove the pasta roll from the water and allow to cool slightly.

Preheat the oven to 180°C (350°F/Gas 4). Unwrap the pasta roll and slice into 2–3 cm (¾ x 1¼ inch) slices and place on a large greased baking tray. Top with the butter and Parmigiano Reggiano cheese and bake for approximately 15–20 minutes, or until light golden. Serve immediately with the butter from the dish spooned over, extra Parmigiano Reggiano cheese and truffle, if desired.

NOTE: *The pasta for this dish needs to be thin, otherwise the middle of the pasta roll will not be cooked. However, if the pasta is too thin, the pasta roll will tear and fall apart when slicing.*

Riggidanella con mortadella e uova sode
Eggplant & pasta bake with mortadella & boiled egg
Serves 6

This is not the classic version of the Calabrian riggidanella. *I have modified the recipe to include two ingredients that I love to use with eggplant in baked dishes: boiled egg and mortadella. It may seem like a curious flavour combination if you have never eaten it before, but it is wonderful, especially when the tomato passata used in the recipe is homemade with very ripe and sweet tomatoes.*

extra virgin olive oil, for shallow-frying

500 g (1 lb 2 oz) eggplant (aubergine), sliced 1 cm (½ inch) thick

250 g (9 oz) good-quality dried short maccheroni pasta, cooked *al dente*

250 ml (9 fl oz/1 cup) good-quality tomato passata (puréed tomatoes)

dried chilli flakes, to taste

120 g (4¼ oz) thinly sliced good-quality mortadella

4 x 59 g (2¼ oz) free-range or organic boiled eggs, sliced

100 g (3½ oz/1 cup) freshly grated pecorino cheese

6 sweet basil leaves, torn

400 ml (14 fl oz) béchamel sauce (page 193)

fine sea salt, to taste

freshly ground black pepper, to taste

Preheat the oven to 180°C (350°F/Gas 4). Heat 1 cm (½ inch) of extra virgin olive oil in a large frying pan over medium heat and fry the eggplant in batches until light golden and soft, turning once. Place on paper towel.

Grease six individual baking dishes, approximately 15 cm (6 inches) in diameter and 3 cm (1¼ inches) high. Line the dishes with the grilled eggplant, with some hanging over the edges for covering later. Mix the cooked pasta and tomato passata together and press into the dishes. Layer the chilli flakes, mortadella, egg, pecorino cheese, basil leaves and béchamel. Fold the overhanging eggplant over the top. Bake for 20 minutes. Serve immediately by turning out onto a plate.

Cannelloni di melanzane e zucchine bianche
Italian eggplant & white zucchini cannelloni
Serves 6

100 ml (3½ fl oz) extra virgin olive oil

350 g (12 oz) Italian eggplant (aubergine), finely diced

350 g (12 oz) medium white zucchini (courgette), finely diced

250 g (9 oz) onion, finely diced

fine sea salt, to taste

freshly ground black pepper, to taste

150 g (5½ oz) fresh ricotta cheese

200 g (7 oz) aged buffalo mozzarella cheese, half sliced and half processed in a food processor to breadcrumb size

150 g (5½ oz/1½ cups) freshly grated Parmigiano Reggiano cheese

750 ml (26 fl oz/3 cups) neapolitan tomato sauce (page 190)

300 g (10½ oz) fresh egg pasta dough (paged 197), rolled into 1 mm (⅟₃₂ inch) lasagne sheets

6 sweet basil leaves, torn

Preheat the oven to 180°C (350°F/Gas 4). Heat the extra virgin olive oil in a frying pan and separately sauté the eggplant, zucchini and onion over medium–high heat for 5–6 minutes or until fully cooked and soft, seasoning to taste. Cool to room temperature then combine with the ricotta, the processed buffalo mozzarella and half of the Parmigiano Reggiano cheese. Add more seasoning with the sea salt and black pepper if required.

To assemble the cannelloni, spoon some of the neapolitan tomato sauce to cover the base of a 24 x 20 x 5 cm (9½ x 8 x 2 inch) ovenproof baking dish. Place the vegetable mixture in a piping (icing) bag with a 2 cm (¾ inch) nozzle and pipe onto one of the pasta sheets. Roll and seal the edge with a little water and cut before placing the cannelloni into the dish. Repeat with the remaining mixture and pasta. Cover with the remaining sauce and place the basil leaves between the cannelloni. Finish with the sliced buffalo mozzarella and remaining Parmigiano Reggiano cheese and bake for 30–40 minutes, or until the cheeses on top of the cannelloni turn a lovely golden colour. Serve hot.

Maccheroni al forno con gorgonzola dolce e prosciutto

Maccheroni cheese with gorgonzola dolce
& San Daniele prosciutto

Serves 6

500 g (1 lb 2 oz) good-quality dried
   short maccheroni pasta
850 ml (28¾ fl oz) béchamel sauce
   (page 193)
fine sea salt, to taste
freshly ground white pepper, to taste
200 g (7 oz) thinly sliced San Daniele
   prosciutto
100 g (3½ oz) emmental cheese,
   thinly sliced
200 g (7 oz) gorgonzola dolce latte
   cheese, crumbled
100 g (3½ oz/1 cup) freshly grated
   Parmigiano Reggiano cheese

Preheat the oven to 180°C (350°F/Gas 4). Cook the pasta in abundant salted boiling water until slightly under *al dente*. Drain the pasta and mix with 700 ml (24 fl oz) of the béchamel sauce and set aside. Check and adjust seasoning of sea salt and white pepper, keeping in mind that the rest of the ingredients are quite salty.

To assemble the maccheroni cheese bake, grease a 24 x 20 x 5 cm (9½ x 8 x 2 inch) ovenproof baking dish. Layer the ingredients much like making a lasagne. Spread half of the pasta and béchamel mix into the base of the dish followed by half of the prosciutto and the emmental cheese. Add the remaining pasta mix, remaining prosciutto and the gorgonzola. Spread the remaining béchamel over the top and finish with the freshly grated Parmigiano Reggiano cheese. Bake for 25–30 minutes or until golden brown on top.

Pasta in Zuppa
Pasta Soups

Dove l'orto era protagonista
The domain of the gardener

Italy is a land of contrasts, a marriage of refinement and the rustic. It does both extremely well, usually simultaneously. As I often say, they have mastered the art of having one foot in a gardening boot and the other in a Salvatore Ferragamo calf-skin shoe.

When I was a student in Italy back in 1992, I remember reading an article in *The European* newspaper on the Italian Federal Parliament. Of course, the Italian Parliament is famous for a lot of things, good and bad, but in this article the author was talking about a curious topic: the fact that many Italian federal politicians maintained their own private vegetable gardens. I can't remember the exact figure, but it was extraordinary, something like over 50 per cent. If you have lived in Italy or know Italians, you will understand and be amused by this. In Italy, gardening is in the blood.

Soup is food from the garden, and the garden is extremely important in all parts of Italy. It is not surprising, then, that every region of Italy specialises in soup. In most cases, soup is *cucina rustica* (rustic cooking) at work, giving an enormous amount of nourishment and satisfaction from simple ingredients. Soups fill us up, warm us up and make us feel good. By definition, soups are simple one-pot meals and most Italians melt before a simple soup done well.

I grew up eating a lot of soups. Most contained some form of pasta and comprised an entire meal.

These types of soups are particularly popular in southern Italy, a legacy of a time much less abundant than the times we live in now. It is ironic that the soup-based diet of my father's youth, packed full of vegetables and legumes and drizzled with fresh extra virgin olive oil, was extremely healthy. They believed that they had a poor diet because it lacked animal protein. Now we are constantly encouraged to move back to a similar, simpler way of eating. Not a bad way to go, in my mind.

And it is funny how things evolve over time, how we are not very interested in certain foods as children and then crave them as adults. This is definitely my experience with these kinds of pasta soups. My mum and dad had to virtually force-feed these soups to me and my brothers Ross and Paul. I can't speak for my brothers, but now I love them all. I believe this process is more than simply a maturing of taste buds; it also has something to do with the connection between memory and emotion. Whichever way you look at it, the soups taste great.

The recipes in this section are hearty and flavoursome one-pot meals, perfect for modern living. I like all of them during the cooler months of the year and also enjoy the lighter broth-based soups, particularly the seafood and fish soups, in spring and even summer.

Zuppa di scampi e spaghetti
Abruzzo-style scampi & spaghetti soup
Serves 6

2½ tablespoons extra virgin olive oil, plus extra for drizzling

1 medium onion, cut into 5 mm (¼ inch) dice

1 medium celery stalk, cut into 5 mm (¼ inch) dice

1 medium carrot, cut into 5 mm (¼ inch) dice

1 sweet bullhorn chilli (pepper), finely diced

1 long red chilli, finely diced

1 garlic clove, finely diced

2 vine-ripened tomatoes, cut into 5 mm (¼ inch) dice

2½ tablespoons dry white wine

2.4 litres (84 fl oz) crustacean broth (page 189)

fine sea salt, to taste

freshly ground black pepper, to taste

300 g (10½ oz) good-quality dried spaghetti

1.2 kg (2 lb 10 oz) fresh scampi, cut in half and cleaned

2 tablespoons chopped flat-leaf (Italian) parsley

Heat the extra virgin olive oil in a large saucepan. Add the onion, celery, carrot, bullhorn chilli, red chilli and garlic and slowly sauté until the onion and garlic become translucent. Add the diced tomato and sauté for a further 5 minutes before adding the white wine. Cook for a further 5 minutes or until the wine has completely evaporated. Add the crustacean broth and bring to the boil, season with the sea salt and black pepper and then slowly simmer for another 15 minutes. The vegetables need to be completely cooked before moving to the next stage of cooking.

Add the dried pasta and cook for approximately 10 minutes or until the pasta is almost fully cooked. Add the scampi and raise the heat. Cook the scampi in the soup for a few minutes, taking care not to overcook them. Stir in the parsley and serve immediately with a drizzle of extra virgin olive oil.

Polpettini in brodo della zia

Auntie Lidia's chicken meatball soup with risoni —the best soup in the world!

Serves 6

A dinner invite from zia Lidia, my auntie, means this soup. I wouldn't have it any other way as it tastes amazing and everyone loves it. She cooks and prepares wonderful food, including the most fantastic pickled artichokes in oil, but this soup is my favourite. During winter, we feature this soup in Caffè Pendolino in Sydney, and it is no surprise that it is always a big hit. At Pendolino, we substitute the risoni for freshly made quadrettini pasta, which is a nice touch, but risoni or pastina are the classic pastas to use.

2.4 litres (84 fl oz) chicken broth
   (page 185)
fine sea salt, to taste
200 g (7 oz) risoni
freshly grated Parmigiano Reggiano
   cheese, to serve (optional)

MEATBALLS

300g (10½ oz) minced (ground)
   chicken
2 x 59 g (2¼ oz) free-range or
   organic eggs
90 g (3¼ oz/1½ cups) fresh white
   breadcrumbs
150 g (5½ oz/1½ cups) freshly grated
   Parmigiano Reggiano cheese
1½ tablespoons finely chopped
   flat-leaf (Italian) parsley
fine sea salt, to taste
freshly ground black pepper, to taste

To make the meatballs, mix all the meatball ingredients together. Roll into balls that are 2.5 cm (1 inch) in diameter and set aside on a plate or tray. My auntie's tip for rolling the meatballs is to lightly cover your hands with olive oil as this makes rolling very easy and prevents the mixture from sticking to your hands.

Bring the chicken broth to the boil. Season with the sea salt, being careful not to overseason as the meatballs will add saltiness to the soup. Add the chicken meatballs one by one. Allow to simmer for 15 minutes before adding the pasta. Cook for about 10 minutes, stirring the risoni intermittently. Serve topped with freshly grated Parmigiano Reggiano cheese, if desired.

Passatelli

Fresh bread & parmesan cheese 'noodles' in chicken broth

Serves 6

150 g (5½ oz/1⅓ cups) dry
    breadcrumbs
150 g (5½ oz/1½ cups) freshly grated
    Parmigiano Reggiano cheese
3 x 59 g (2¼ oz) free-range
    or organic eggs
freshly grated nutmeg, to taste
fine sea salt, to taste
2.4 litres (84 fl oz) chicken broth
    (page 185)

In a medium-sized bowl, combine the breadcrumbs and Parmigiano Reggiano cheese and mix well. Form a hole in the mixture and break the eggs into it. Grate the desired amount of nutmeg into the egg and add a little sea salt for seasoning. Mix the egg with a fork or your fingers and then bring all the ingredients together to form a homogenous wet dough. Place this into a potato ricer and set aside.

Bring the chicken broth to the boil. Add a little sea salt if required. Push some of the dough through the potato ricer to form 'noodles' and cut them with a knife to form lengths of about 4 cm (1½ inches). They should be cut directly into the boiling broth. The broth will lose heat at first but will come back to the boil quickly. Cook for about 3 minutes and serve immediately.

Pasta e fagioli
Pasta with dried cannellini beans
Serves 6

Nowadays, particularly outside of Italy, there is a lot of reference to 'regional Italian cooking' rather than 'Italian cooking'. Anyone acquainted with the food of Italy will know that regional differences are usually distinct, and I am the first to agree with this. I also believe that there is something that intrinsically ties the 20 regions of Italy together to make Italian cooking distinct from other cuisines. It is cultural and hard to identify, but pasta and flavour are central to the discussion. **Pasta e fagioli** *is a dish that you will find in nearly every part of Italy and it will be very similar in each place. To most Italians, it is as simple as food can be, and almost as endearing as a long lost friend. Enjoy this dish on a cold, wet winter's day, drizzled with very good extra virgin olive oil and served with lots of freshly grated Parmigiano Reggiano or pecorino cheese. A glass of Sangiovese or similar medium-bodied red wine will make the experience sublime.*

2½ tablespoons extra virgin olive oil, plus extra for drizzling

1 medium onion, cut into 5 mm (¼ inch) dice

1 medium celery stalk, cut into 5 mm (¼ inch) dice

1 garlic clove, finely chopped

250 g (9 oz) dried cannellini beans, soaked in water overnight

approximately 3 litres (105 fl oz/12 cups) water or vegetable broth (page 187)

fine sea salt, to taste

2 medium potatoes, cut into 5 mm (¼ inch) dice

1 rosemary sprig, broken into pieces

250 g (9 oz) good-quality dried conchigliette (small shell) pasta

freshly ground black pepper, to serve

dried chilli flakes, to serve

freshly grated Parmigiano Reggiano or pecorino cheese, to serve

Heat the extra virgin olive oil in a large saucepan. Add the onion, celery and garlic and slowly sauté until the vegetables become translucent. Drain the soaked cannellini beans and add to the pan with enough water or vegetable broth to cover the beans by about 4 cm (1½ inches). Bring to the boil, season with the sea salt and let simmer for 30 minutes. After about 30 minutes of cooking, add the potato and rosemary and slowly simmer until the beans are well cooked. If the water level is reducing too far, you can add a little more water or vegetable broth until the desired level is reached. Sometimes I substitute the water or vegetable broth for chicken broth as it gives the soup a little more flavour, but it is definitely not necessary.

Bring a medium-sized saucepan full of salted water to the boil and cook the pasta. As it is a soup, cook the pasta a little past the *al dente* point. Strain the pasta and add to the soup then serve with freshly ground black pepper, dried chilli flakes, a drizzle of extra virgin olive oil and freshly grated Parmigiano Reggiano or pecorino cheese.

Brodetto all'anconetana con sagnette e bastardone

Classic Ancona-style seafood broth with sagnette & dried 'big bastard' chilli

Serves 6

2½ tablespoons extra virgin olive oil, plus extra for drizzling

1 medium onion, cut into 5 mm (¼ inch) dice

1 medium celery stalk, cut into 5 mm (¼ inch) dice

1 medium carrot, cut into 5 mm (¼ inch) dice

1 garlic clove, finely chopped

2½ tablespoons white wine vinegar

1.8 litres (63 fl oz) crustacean broth (page 189)

500 ml (17 fl oz/2 cups) good-quality tomato passata (puréed tomatoes)

fine sea salt, to taste

freshly ground black pepper, to taste

1 medium potato, cut into 5 mm (¼ inch) dice

200 g (7 oz) good-quality dried sagnette pasta (see Note)

600 g (1 lb 5 oz) mixed cleaned and prepared fish and shellfish (such as prawns (shrimp), calamari, squid, clams, mussels, scorpion fish, scallops, scampi, snapper), cut into bite-sized pieces

2 tablespoons chopped flat-leaf (Italian) parsley

6 slices Italian bread, toasted and rubbed with garlic

6 very large dried red chillies

Heat the extra virgin olive oil in a large saucepan. Add the onion, celery, carrot and garlic and slowly sauté until the onion and garlic become translucent. Raise the heat and add the vinegar. Cook for a few minutes before adding the crustacean broth and tomato passata. Bring to the boil and season with the sea salt and black pepper. Add the potato and then slowly simmer for 20 minutes. Add the dried pasta and cook for a further 8–12 minutes or until the pasta is fully cooked. Add the seafood and raise the heat. Be sure to add the clams first and cook for a minute before adding the rest of the seafood. Cook for a few minutes until all the mussels and clams have opened. Be careful not to overcook the fish. Stir in the parsley and serve by placing the toasted bread and the dried chilli on top of the soup. Complete by drizzling extra virgin olive oil over the bread and into the soup. Serve immediately.

NOTE: *Sagnette pasta is roughly the thickness of tagliatelle and about 7 cm (2¾ inches) long. Broken tagliatelle and linguini are good substitutes.*

Brodo di coda di bue con quadretti e funghi di bosco

Oxtail broth with fresh pasta squares & dried wild forest mushrooms

Serves 6

250 g (9 oz) fresh egg pasta
dough (page 197)

25 g (1 oz) mixed dried wild
mushrooms

2.4 litres (84 fl oz) oxtail broth
(page 186)

450 g (1 lb) braised oxtail meat
(from oxtail broth recipe on
page 186)

fine sea salt, to taste

freshly ground black pepper, to taste

200 g (7 oz) fresh small exotic
mushrooms, to garnish

freshly grated Parmigiano Reggiano
cheese, to serve

Roll the pasta dough into sheets of 1 mm (1/32 inch) thickness. Cut the pasta into 2 x 2 cm (3/4 x 3/4 inch) squares. A corrugated roller cutter is best for this job as it makes wonderful jagged-edged squares.

Cover the dried mushrooms with boiling water and leave for 15 minutes until the water has cooled and the mushrooms have settled to the top (see Note). Lift the mushrooms out of the water and set aside.

Bring the oxtail broth to the boil. Add the soaked mushrooms, braised oxtail meat and a little sea salt and black pepper, if required, and simmer for approximately 20 minutes. Add the pasta squares and cook for 3–4 minutes. Serve immediately garnished with the exotic mushrooms and lots of freshly grated Parmigiano Reggiano cheese.

NOTE: *Soaking the mushrooms is essential as dried mushroom products tend to contain dirt and grit. Lifting the mushrooms out of the water instead of pouring everything through a sieve helps to ensure the dirt is properly removed. Repeat the process of submerging the mushrooms in water if they contain a lot of grit.*

Ditalini con lenticchie di castelluccio e guanciale
Ditalini with castelluccio lentils & cured pork cheek

Serves 6

2½ tablespoons extra virgin olive oil,
  plus extra for drizzling
1 medium onion, cut into 5 mm
  (¼ inch) dice
1 medium celery stalk, cut into 5 mm
  (¼ inch) dice
1 medium carrot, cut into 5 mm
  (¼ inch) dice
300 g (10 ½ oz) diced guanciale
  (pancetta is a good substitute)
2 garlic cloves, finely chopped
250 g (9 oz) dried castelluccio lentils
  or brown lentils
1 litre (35 fl oz/4 cups) chicken broth
  (page 185)
250 ml (9 fl oz/1 cup) good-quality
  tomato passata (puréed tomatoes)
fine sea salt, to taste
freshly ground black pepper, to taste
200 g (7 oz) good-quality dried
  ditalini pasta
2 tablespoons chopped flat-leaf
  (Italian) parsley
freshly grated Parmigiano Reggiano
  or pecorino cheese, to serve
6 slices Italian casareccio bread

Heat the extra virgin olive oil in a large saucepan. Add the onion, celery, carrot, guanciale and garlic and slowly sauté until the onion and garlic become translucent. Add the lentils, chicken broth and tomato passata to the pan. Bring to the boil, season with the sea salt and black pepper, then cover and cook slowly for about 50–60 minutes or until the lentils are tender.

Bring a medium-sized saucepan full of salted water to the boil and cook the ditalini pasta. As this is a soup, the pasta should be cooked slightly beyond *al dente*. Add the pasta to the soup and mix well. Add the parsley and season further with the sea salt and freshly ground black pepper to taste. Serve with the freshly grated Parmigiano Reggiano or pecorino cheese. Complete by placing the bread on the soup and drizzling the extra virgin olive oil over the bread and into the soup. Serve immediately.

Lumachoni con cime di rapa e peperoncino

Large snail pasta with broccoli rabe, dried chilli & pecorino cheese

Serves 6

2½ tablespoons extra virgin olive oil, plus extra, to serve

1 garlic clove, finely chopped

4 vine-ripened tomatoes, cored and diced

2.4 litres (84 fl oz) hot vegetable broth (page 187)

450 g (1 lb) cime di rapa (broccoli rabe), stems removed, washed and roughly chopped into bite-sized pieces (see Note)

2 medium potatoes, cut into 5 mm (¼ inch) dice

250 g (9 oz) good-quality dried lumachoni pasta

fine sea salt, to taste

freshly grated pecorino cheese, to serve

dried chilli flakes, to taste

freshly ground black pepper, to taste

Heat the extra virgin olive oil in a large saucepan. Add the garlic and slowly sauté for a few seconds before adding the tomato, taking care not to burn the garlic. Continue to sauté for about 5 minutes. Add the hot vegetable broth and then the cime di rapa and potato. Bring to the boil and cook for a further 15 minutes. Add the lumachoni pasta and cook for approximately 12 minutes or until the pasta is fully cooked. Add the sea salt to taste. Serve immediately with lots of extra virgin olive oil and freshly grated pecorino cheese. Add the dried chilli flakes and freshly ground black pepper to taste.

NOTE: *If cime di rapa (broccoli rabe) is unavailable, you can substitute it with any similar bitter green leaf, such as chicory or curly endive.*

Cuscus con zuppa di pesce
Trapani seafood soup with couscous

Serves 6

6 clams (vongole)

6 mussels

400 g (14 oz) baby squid

2½ tablespoons extra virgin olive oil,
plus extra for drizzling

2 medium onions, cut into 5 mm
(¼ inch) dice

2 garlic cloves, finely chopped

4 vine-ripened tomatoes, cut into
5 mm (¼ inch) dice, reserving
the juices

2 litres (70 fl oz/8 cups) fish broth
(page 186)

fine sea salt, to taste

freshly ground black pepper, to taste

300 g (10½ oz) couscous

12 large scallops

200 g (7 oz) white-fleshed fish,
such as snapper, cut into
2–3 cm (¾–1¼ inch) dice

2 tablespoons chopped flat-leaf
(Italian) parsley

If they haven't been purged, place the clams in a solution of cool water and sea salt for several hours or overnight in a cool part of the house (if you refrigerate them, they'll close up and won't 'spit out' the sand). As a guide, use 30 g (1 oz) of salt for each 1 litre (35 fl oz/4 cups) of water.

To prepare the mussels, lightly scrub away the dirt and barnacles on the shell and 'de-beard' by pulling away the hairy tendrils entering the shell. To prepare the squid, pull the insides out and trim away the tops, cutting just above the tentacles. Discard the 'spine' from inside the squid. Cut along the side of the squid and lay flat, scoring with a knife and chopping into bite-sized pieces.

Heat the extra virgin olive oil in a saucepan over medium–low heat. Add the onion and half of the garlic and slowly sauté until they become translucent. Raise the heat and add the tomato. Add the fish broth, bring to the boil, season with the sea salt and black pepper and then slowly simmer for 30 minutes. While this is cooking, prepare the couscous by placing it in a deep bowl and covering it with salted hot water. Cover the bowl with a lid or plastic wrap and set aside for 10 minutes.

Meanwhile, add the seafood to the broth and raise the heat. Be sure to add the mussels and clams first to let them cook for a minute before adding the rest of the seafood as they take a little longer to cook. Cook the seafood for a few minutes until all the mussels and clams have opened. Be careful not to overcook the fish. Stir in the parsley and remaining garlic. Run a fork through the couscous to separate the grains and spoon into the bottom of a deep soup bowl. Place the soup on top and finish with a generous drizzle of extra virgin olive oil.

Farfalle con broccoli e ceci
Butterfly pasta with broccoli & chickpeas
Serves 6

2½ tablespoons extra virgin olive oil,
   plus extra for drizzling
1 garlic clove, peeled and crushed
   with the flat edge of a knife
300 g (10½ oz/1½ cups) dried
   chickpeas, soaked in water
   overnight and drained
3 litres (105 fl oz/12 cups) chicken
   broth (page 185) reduced to
   2.5 litres (87 fl oz/10 cups)
200 g (7 oz) good-quality dried
   farfalle pasta
300 g (10½ oz) broccoli florettes
fine sea salt, to taste
freshly ground black pepper, to serve
freshly grated Parmigiano Reggiano
   cheese, to serve

Heat the extra virgin olive oil in a large saucepan and sauté the garlic until it turns a golden brown colour. Add the chickpeas and chicken broth and bring to the boil. Once boiling, lower the heat and simmer until the chickpeas are fully cooked. Add the pasta and cook for about 10 minutes. Add the broccoli and cook for a few more minutes. Take care not to overcook the broccoli. It needs to be cooked to the point where it is tender but still has a vibrant green colour. Add the sea salt to taste. Serve immediately with the freshly ground black pepper, a drizzle of extra virgin olive oil and the freshly grated Parmigiano Reggiano cheese.

Ruote con minestra di rigaglie di pollo
Little wheel pasta with chicken giblet soup

Serves 6

I adore this dish. Just writing about it makes me feel a great sense of nostalgia. It reminds me of my youth when my father would go hunting and we would eat wild duck giblets soup in the days following the hunt. Wild duck giblets are great in this soup, but not easy to obtain for most people. Chicken giblets are a great substitute as they also have wonderful flavour with a slightly 'chewy' texture that characterises all giblets. When cooked in broth for the right amount of time, the giblets become beautifully tender. Nowadays, chicken giblets are not very popular and in my opinion they are vastly underrated. Enjoy them in this wonderful soup.

2½ tablespoons extra virgin olive oil

1 medium onion, cut into 5 mm (¼ inch) dice

1 medium celery stalk, cut into 5 mm (¼ inch) dice

1 medium carrot, cut into 5 mm (¼ inch) dice

1 garlic clove, finely chopped

500 g (1 lb 2 oz) cleaned chicken giblets (see Note)

3 litres (105 fl oz/12 cups) chicken broth (page 185)

fine sea salt, to taste

1 medium potato, cut into 5 mm (¼ inch) dice

200 g (7 oz) good-quality ruote (little wheel) dried pasta

2 tablespoons chopped flat-leaf (Italian) parsley

freshly grated Parmigiano Reggiano cheese, to serve

Heat the extra virgin olive oil in a large saucepan. Add the onion, celery, carrot and garlic and slowly sauté until the onion and garlic become translucent. Add the chicken giblets and continue to sauté for another 5 minutes before adding the chicken broth. Bring to the boil, season with the sea salt, and let simmer for 2–3 hours or until the giblets become tender. Add the potato and simmer until the potato is fully cooked. Add the pasta and cook for 10–12 minutes. Just before serving, stir in the chopped parsley and serve with lots of freshly grated Parmigiano Reggiano cheese.

NOTE: *Order the giblets in advance from your butcher and ask them to trim and clean them well for you. As a guide, 800 g (1 lb 12 oz) of untrimmed giblets will yield 500 g (1 lb 2 oz).*

Brodo di stinco di vitello con orzo e conchiglie
Veal shank soup with pearl barley, shell pasta & leek
Serves 6

100 ml (3½ fl oz) extra virgin olive oil

2 leeks, cut into 5 mm (¼ inch) dice

1 garlic clove, finely chopped

450 g (1 lb) veal shank

fine sea salt, to taste

freshly ground black pepper, to taste

3 litres (105 fl oz/12 cups) veal or
   beef broth (page 187)

1 small bay leaf

1 thyme sprig

200 g (7 oz/1 cup) pearl barley

200 g (7 oz) conchiglie dried pasta

2 tablespoons chopped flat-leaf
   (Italian) parsley

freshly grated Parmigiano Reggiano
   cheese, to serve

Heat half of the extra virgin olive oil in a large saucepan. Add the leek and garlic and slowly sauté until the vegetables become translucent. Season the veal shank with the sea salt and black pepper and pour the remaining extra virgin olive oil into a separate frying pan. Brown the veal shank in this pan, taking care not to burn it, before placing it in the pan with the leek and garlic. Add the broth, bay leaf, thyme and pearl barley and bring to the boil. Adjust the seasoning if required and let simmer for 2–3 hours or until the meat on the veal shank begins to fall off the bone. Stir regularly to prevent the barley from sticking to the base of the pan and burning.

When the meat is fully cooked, remove it from the pot and allow to cool before removing all the meat from the bone. Break or cut the meat up into bite-sized pieces and return to the soup. Bring the soup to the boil, add the pasta and cook for 10–12 minutes. Just before serving, stir in the parsley and serve with lots of freshly grated Parmigiano Reggiano cheese.

Tortellini bolognese in brodo di capone
Meat tortellini in capon broth

Serves 6

900 ml (31½ fl oz) capon broth
(see Note) or chicken broth
(page 185)
fine sea salt, to taste
600 g (1 lb 5 oz) meat tortellini
(see meat tortellini with classic
bolognaise sauce on page 93)
freshly grated Parmigiano Reggiano
cheese, to taste

In a large saucepan, bring the capon or chicken broth to the boil. Add a little sea salt, if required. Add the tortellini and cook for about 10 minutes. The tortellini will be ready when they float to the top. Serve the tortellini and broth with lots of freshly grated Parmigiano Reggiano cheese.

NOTE: *The use of castrated roosters, or capons, is widespread in Italy, but they are particularly prized in Emilia-Romagna where they are celebrated in one of the region's most famous dishes—tortellini in brodo. The process of castration enables roosters to develop extremely flavoursome meat that is ideal for making broths. As capon is unavailable in many places like Australia, the broth recipe that I use calls for a whole boiling hen and the addition of chicken bones to strengthen the intensity of the broth flavour.*

Pasta Dolce

Dessert Pasta

La pasta può essere un dolce?
Can pasta be a dessert?

It probably seems strange to include desserts in a pasta cookbook. It may seem stranger still to say that this is far from being an exercise in experimental modern Italian cooking. In fact, this section of the book contains some of the book's most traditional pasta recipes.

This isn't unusual if you consider what pasta really means and how it is used in a wide variety of ways to make desserts and sweet dishes in Italian cooking. In literal terms, pasta simply means 'pastry'. Consider the Italian culinary terms *pasta frolla* (shortcrust pastry) and *pasta sfoglia* (puff pastry). Pasta eaten as a savoury dish is so dominant in Italy and abroad that most of the world only knows the word to mean 'pasta' and not 'pastry'. The recipes in this section, however, do not contain puff or shortcrust pastry; they are pasta as we know it, or very close variations, and they are sweet.

Pasta in desserts goes back a long, long way, for as long as pastry desserts have been made in Italy. And in some places the definition of sweet and savoury is significantly blurred. Take the extraordinary dish from Friuli Venezia Giulia known as *gnocchi di susine:* small sugar (president) plums wrapped in a potato gnocchi dough then gently boiled before being served with fine breadcrumbs fried in butter and a dusting of sugar. The dish is unmistakably pasta, but it looks and tastes like a dessert, and it has been eaten for centuries as a main meal during times of fasting in a way that savoury pasta dishes are usually eaten. Not really fasting food, you might say. Well, I would agree! In spite of this, it doesn't contain meat and is full of energy, which makes it a perfect Lenten meal for people in mountain regions involved in high-energy manual labour.

At the other end of Italy we find recipes like *pignolata*, which is from my father's region, Calabria. It is a very simple adaptation of the basic pasta dough recipe, only it is sweet, fried and served with honey. Like *gnocchi di susine*, this dish was also eaten as part of ritual celebrations at Easter.

These pasta dessert recipes are all wonderful. Enjoy them!

Cjalsons (agnolotti) friulani
Friulan potato dough agnolotti
Makes approximately 40 agnolotti

300 g (10½ oz) starchy potatoes,
   such as bintje or pink eye
300 g (10½ oz/2 cups) plain
   (all-purpose) flour
1 tablespoon extra virgin olive oil
2½ tablespoons lukewarm water
1 x 59 g (2¼ oz) free-range
   or organic egg
150 g (5½ oz) salted butter, chopped
100 g (3½ oz/½ cup) brown sugar
olive oil, for deep-frying
icing (confectioners') sugar,
   for dusting
6 scoops of vanilla bean ice cream,
   to serve

FILLING

50 g (1¾ oz) dark bitter chocolate,
   grated
40 g (1½ oz/⅓ cup) walnuts, chopped
40 g (1½ oz) candied fruit, finely
   chopped
150 g (5½ oz) fresh ricotta cheese
50 g (1¾ oz) pitted prunes, finely
   chopped
50 g (1¾ oz) dried figs, finely
   chopped
1 teaspoon grated lemon zest
1 tablespoon grappa
1 vanilla bean, split lengthways
   and seeds scraped
1 teaspoon ground cinnamon,
   or to taste
1 tablespoon honey

To prepare the potatoes, boil them with the skin on until soft. Peel the skin off the potatoes while hot and pass through a food mill or potato ricer. Combine the potatoes and flour in a large bowl. Add the oil and water and combine until a smooth dough is formed. Rest for 30–60 minutes.

For the filling, mix all the ingredients in a large bowl until well incorporated. Set aside.

To make the cjalsons, roll out the dough to about 2 mm (1⁄16 inch) thickness on a lightly floured surface. Using a pastry cutter, cut the dough into round discs roughly 10 cm (4 inches) in diameter. Place a spoonful of filling on each of the discs and then fold over to the edge to form a half-moon, making sure to remove as much air as possible. Press the edges down with a fork and trim with a slightly smaller cutter. Beat the egg and use a pastry brush to glaze the top of each cjalson.

To make the sauce, place the butter and sugar in a small saucepan over low heat and stir constantly until the brown sugar has dissolved and the sauce is a smooth consistency.

In a saucepan or deep frying pan, heat about 5 cm (2 inches) of olive oil to 180°C (350°F) and deep-fry the cjalsons in batches for about 4 minutes or until golden and crispy. Drain on a paper towel. Dust with icing sugar and serve hot with the ice cream and prepared sauce.

Caggionetti al mosto di montepulciano
Abbruzzese fried sweet ravioli

Makes 40–50 ravioli

150 g (5½ oz) dried chestnuts

300 ml (10½ fl oz) mosto cotto (vino cotto) from Montepulciano red wine grapes (see Note)

150 g (5½ oz) blanched almonds, toasted and crushed

60 g (2¼ oz) dark bitter chocolate, grated

50 g (1¾ oz) caster (superfine) sugar

1 vanilla bean, split lengthways and seeds scraped

15 ml (½ fl oz) anisette (aniseed liqueur)

15 ml (½ fl oz) dark rum

300 g (10½ oz/2 cups) plain (all-purpose) flour

90 ml (3 fl oz) extra virgin olive oil

90 ml (3 fl oz) Trebbiano white wine or similar (a soft-bodied Pinot Grigio is a suitable replacement)

olive oil, for deep-frying

icing (confectioners') sugar, for dusting

ground cinnamon, for dusting

Soak the dried chestnuts in water overnight. Strain and place in a saucepan covered with water. Boil until tender. Drain and pass through a strainer or food mill. Weigh out 150 g (5½ oz). Set aside.

Heat the mosto cotto in a saucepan over low heat and stir in the almonds, chocolate, caster sugar, vanilla bean seeds, anisette and rum until the chocolate has melted. Add the chestnut purée and mix until smooth. Refrigerate until cooled.

Make a mound of the flour on your work surface and scoop a hole out of the middle to make a well. Mix in the extra virgin olive oil and wine to obtain a firm, elastic dough. You're aiming for something that has the consistency of pasta dough, so it's going to be considerably firmer than bread dough. Knead the dough well and divide it into two parts. On a lightly floured work surface, roll out the first portion into a thin sheet about 2 mm (1/16 inch) thick. Use a circular pastry cutter to cut out 5 cm (2 inch) diameter rounds of dough. In the middle of each round, place a hazelnut-sized chunk of filling, then fold the pasta over the filling and tamp it down well to obtain bulging half-moons. Repeat the process with the second piece of dough and the cuttings from the first.

Heat the olive oil in a deep saucepan, no more than half full, to 180°C (350°F) and deep-fry the caggionetti in batches for about 4 minutes. As soon as they're golden, remove with a slotted spoon and drain them on a paper towel. Dust them with the icing sugar and cinnamon and serve hot.

NOTE: *Any vino cotto product will be a good substitute.*

Gnocchi di susine

Friulan plum gnocchi

Serves 6

600 g (1 lb 5 oz) potato gnocchi
    dough (page 212)
12 sugar (president) plums, deseeded
3 tablespoons dark brown sugar
100 g (3½ oz) salted butter
30 g (1 oz/½ cup) fresh white
    breadcrumbs
1 teaspoon ground cinnamon,
    plus extra for dusting
1 vanilla bean, split lengthways
    and seeds scraped
icing (confectioners') sugar,
    for dusting

On a lightly floured work surface, roll out the gnocchi dough to 2–3 mm (1/16 x 1/8 inch) thickness and cut into 12 discs large enough to completely wrap your plums. Place a plum on each of the discs and put ½ teaspoon of the dark brown sugar in the centre of the plum. Wrap the dough around the plum to completely cover it to form a large *gnocco* (dumpling). Make sure there are no holes in the dough. Repeat this process for all 12 plums. Excess dough can be re-rolled to make more gnocchi.

Heat the butter in a saucepan and brown the breadcrumbs over medium heat. Strain the butter and set aside in a warm place. Place breadcrumbs on a paper towel to drain until dry. When drained, add the cinnamon, remaining dark brown sugar and vanilla bean seeds and mix together.

Boil the gnocchi in salted water until they come to the surface. Remove with a slotted spoon and rest on a tea towel (dish towel) so that most of the water drains from the gnocchi. Roll the gnocchi in the prepared breadcrumb, cinnamon, sugar and vanilla mixture and place two gnocchi on each plate. Drizzle some of the strained browned butter over the top. Dust with the icing sugar and extra cinnamon and serve.

Crostoli

Fried pasta ribbons

Makes approximately 26 pasta ribbons

These beautiful pastries are found almost everywhere in Italy in some form. They are extremely versatile and are a great accompaniment for coffee or ice-cream-based desserts.

350 g (12 oz/2⅓ cup) plain
   (all-purpose) flour
50 g (1¾ oz) caster (superfine) sugar
1 teaspoon baking powder
a pinch of fine sea salt
60 g (2¼ oz) unsalted butter
   (at room temperature)
2 free-range or organic egg yolks
90 ml (3 fl oz) grappa
2 tablespoons full-cream (whole) milk
olive oil, for deep-frying
icing (confectioners') sugar, for dusting

Reserve 2 tablespoons of the flour. Put the rest of the flour in a bowl and combine with the caster sugar, baking powder and sea salt. Add the butter, egg yolks, grappa and milk. Mix all the ingredients together by hand until a dough is formed. If the dough is too dry, add a little more milk. If the dough is too wet, add extra flour. Knead for at least 5 minutes. The dough should be smooth and elastic. Rest for at least 1 hour, then roll by hand on a lightly floured work surface to 1 mm (1/32 inch) thickness. This can also be done through a pasta machine, but extra flour will be needed for dusting between rolls. Cut into strips, roughly the width of a wooden ruler and 19 cm (7½ inches) in length, with a jagged-edged ravioli cutter. Re-roll the offcuts if desired.

Heat the olive oil in a deep saucepan, no more than half full, to 180°C (350°F) and then deep-fry the crostoli for about 3 minutes or until golden and puffy. Drain on a paper towel and dust with the icing sugar to serve.

Gnocchetti fritti all'uva moscato
Fried sweet baby gnocchi with dried muscatels

Serves 6

This sweet fried pasta dish is very rich and usually served in small quantities, as with biscuits or petit fours. It is wonderful with fresh coffee and Italian liqueurs.

375 g (13 oz/2½ cups) plain
   (all-purpose) flour
50 g (1¾ oz) brown sugar
140 ml (4½ fl oz) moscato wine
180 ml (5¾ fl oz) extra virgin olive oil
olive oil, for deep-frying

SAUCE

1 vanilla bean, split lengthways
   and seeds scraped
juice of four oranges, strained
100 ml (3½ fl oz) blood orange
   agrumato olive oil (see Note)
100 ml (3½ fl oz) cognac
100 g (3½ oz) dried muscatel
   grapes, deseeded
1 cinnamon stick
1 star anise

Combine the flour and brown sugar on a work surface or large wooden board, add the moscato wine and extra virgin olive oil and bring together. Knead for 5 minutes. Allow to rest for 1 hour. With damp hands, roll the dough into long logs approximately 1 cm (½ inch) in diameter. Cut the logs into 1 cm (½ inch) pieces and roll into little balls.

For the sauce, place all the sauce ingredients in a small saucepan over very low heat, stirring regularly for approximately 15–20 minutes until the muscatels are rehydrated and infused.

Heat the olive oil in a deep saucepan, no more than half full, in a large deep-sided frying pan to 180°C (350°F). Deep-fry the gnocchetti for about 4 minutes or until lightly golden. Drain on a paper towel. Just before serving, toss the gnocchetti through the sauce and serve immediately.

NOTE: *If you can't find blood orange agrumato olive oil, substitute with extra virgin olive oil and half a teaspoon of finely chopped orange zest.*

Ravioli dolci di mela cotogna

Bolognese quince jam ravioli

Makes approximately 26 ravioli

375 g (13 oz/2½ cups) plain
  (all-purpose) flour
110 g (3¾ oz) chilled unsalted butter
  or rendered lard, chopped
75 g (2½ oz/⅓ cup) caster
  (superfine) sugar
100 ml (3½ fl oz) full-cream (whole)
  milk
2 x 59 g (2¼ oz) free-range
  or organic eggs, beaten
a pinch of fine sea salt
icing (confectioners') sugar, to dust
ground cinnamon, to taste

QUINCE JAM

250 g (9 oz) whole quinces
125 ml (4 fl oz/½ cup) water
juice of ½ lemon
175 g (6 oz) caster (superfine) sugar
125 ml (4 fl oz/½ cup) dry Italian
  white wine
½ cinnamon stick
½ vanilla bean

To make the quince jam, wash, peel and core the quinces. Cut them into pieces roughly 3 x 3 cm (1¼ x 1¼ inches) and place them directly into a bowl of water. Before doing this, add half of the lemon juice into the water. This will stop the quinces from discolouring. Drain the quince pieces and place in a small deep saucepan. Add all other quince jam ingredients except the vanilla bean and begin to cook over medium heat. Slice the vanilla bean lengthways and scrape the seeds from the bean with a blunt knife or spoon. Add both the vanilla seeds and the bean pod to the pan and continue to cook. Cover with a cartouche (see Note on page 78). Reduce heat and cook slowly, stirring occasionally for 2 hours or until the quinces become soft. Remove the cinammon stick and vanilla bean pod. Process the mixture in a food processor or food mill. Cool to room temperature.

To make the pastry, combine the flour, butter and caster sugar into a crumbly mix, then add the milk, three-quarters of the beaten egg and a pinch of the sea salt to form a nicely worked short-crust dough. Divide the dough into 3 balls, wrap in plastic wrap and allow to rest in the refrigerator for 30 minutes.

Preheat the oven to 180°C (350°F/Gas 4). Roll out the dough to about 2 mm (1/16 inch) thickness. Using a pastry cutter, cut into round discs roughly 10 cm (4 inches) in diameter. Place ½ a tablespoon of quince jam on each of the discs and then fold over to the edge to form half-moons. Press the edges down with a fork to seal properly. Re-roll offcuts if desired. Use a pastry brush to glaze each ravioli with the remaining beaten egg. Place on trays lined with non-stick baking paper. Bake for about 20–30 minutes. They are fantastic served warm or cold, dusted with icing sugar and cinnamon.

Maccheroni dolci con le noci
Umbrian Christmas macaroni with walnuts
Serves 6

This dish, traditionally served on Christmas Eve, is quite bizarre for anyone outside of Umbria. As a variation on the recipe, I like to serve the dish a little warmer, with the addition of vanilla bean gelato. Either way, it's a fantastic dish, particularly for nut lovers.

100 g (3½ oz) day-old bread, pulsed in a food processor to thick breadcrumbs
100 g (3½ oz) unsalted butter
375 g (13 oz/3¼ cups) roasted walnuts, semi-crushed
75 g (2½ oz/⅓ cup) brown sugar
25 g (1 oz) icing (confectioners') sugar, sifted
25 g (1 oz) premium quality cocoa powder, sifted
150 g (5½ oz) good-quality dried short maccheroni pasta
1 tablespoon walnut oil
1 tablespoon honey

Fry the breadcrumbs in the butter in a frying pan until golden. Strain the butter from the breadcrumbs after frying. Combine the breadcrumbs with the walnuts, brown sugar, icing sugar and cocoa powder. Set aside.

Cook the pasta in abundant salted boiling water until *al dente*. Before straining, pour some cold water on the pasta to cool it down a little. Add the walnut oil and honey and mix through the pasta. Stir through the prepared breadcrumb mixture. Serve at room temperature.

Ravioli dolci di ricotta

Baked sweet ricotta ravioli

Makes approximately 40 ravioli

750 g (1 lb 10 oz/5 cups) plain
(all-purpose) flour

225 g (8 oz) chilled unsalted butter
or lard, chopped

150 g (5½ oz/⅔ cup) caster
(superfine) sugar

225 ml (7¾ fl oz) full-cream
(whole) milk

2 x 59 g (2¼ oz) free-range
or organic eggs, plus 1 extra
for glazing

a pinch of fine sea salt

1 tablespoon icing (confectioners')
sugar, for dusting

1 teaspoon ground cinnamon,
for dusting

FILLING

500 g (1 lb 2 oz) fresh ricotta cheese

150 g (5½ oz) icing (confectioners')
sugar, sifted

3 x 59 g (2¼ oz) free-range
or organic eggs

1 teaspoon ground cinnamon

1 tablespoon chopped sicilian
candied fruit

Combine the flour, butter and caster sugar in a large bowl and mix with your fingertips until it is crumbly. Add the milk and eggs with a pinch of the sea salt to form a nicely worked dough. Divide the dough into two pieces and flatten into discs. Wrap in plastic wrap and allow to rest in the refrigerator for about 1 hour.

Combine all the ingredients for the filling and set aside.

Preheat the oven to 160°C (315°F/Gas 2–3). Roll out the dough on a lightly floured work surface to about 2 mm (¹⁄₁₆ inch) in thickness. Using a pastry cutter, cut into round discs roughly 10 cm (4 inches) in diameter. Place 1 tablespoon of the ricotta mixture on each of the discs and fold over to the edge to form half-moons, making sure to remove as much air as possible. Press the edges down with a fork and trim with a slightly smaller cutter. Re-roll offcuts and continue. Beat the extra egg and use a pastry brush to glaze each ravioli. Place on baking trays lined with non-stick baking paper. Bake for approximately 40–45 minutes or until golden brown. Serve cold dusted with the icing sugar and cinnamon.

Sgonfiotti alla frutta
Alto Adige-style sweet fruit ravioli

Makes approximately 40 ravioli

150 g (5½ oz) chestnuts

200 g (7 oz/1⅓ cups) plain (all-purpose) flour, plus extra, if needed

100 g (3½ oz) rye flour

120 g (4¼ oz) unsalted butter, softened

1 x 59 g (2¼ oz) free-range or organic egg

3 tablespoons cream (pouring), plus extra, if required

a pinch of fine sea salt

1½ tablespoons red currant jelly

150 g (5½ oz/¾ cup) grated peeled apple

20 g (¾ oz/⅓ cup) fresh breadcrumbs

olive oil, for frying

icing sugar, for dusting

Use a sharp knife to cut a cross in the top of each chestnut and place in a small saucepan. Cover with water and boil for 20 minutes or until tender all the way through. Peel the chestnuts while still warm and mash with a potato masher. Set aside.

Combine the flours and butter in a large bowl with your fingertips until crumbly. Add the egg and cream with a pinch of sea salt to form a nicely worked shortcrust dough (see Note). Wrap in plastic wrap and allow to rest in the refrigerator for about an hour.

Prepare the filling by combining the red currant jelly, apple, chestnuts and breadcrumbs. On a lightly floured work surface, roll out the dough to form a very thin sheet, about 2 mm (1/16 inch) thick. Cut 5–7.5 cm (2–3 inch) rounds out of the rolled dough using a pastry cutter. Place a large teaspoonful of the filling in the middle and fold over to form large half-moon ravioli. Press with a fork to reinforce the seal. Repeat until the dough or filling have run out. Re-roll offcuts if desired. Heat 2.5 cm (1 inch) of olive oil in a deep-sided frying pan over medium–high heat and fry the ravioli in batches for about 4 minutes or until golden. Drain on paper towels, dust with icing sugar and serve hot.

NOTE: *Due to the lack of gluten in rye flour, you will need to knead this dough for a lot longer before you allow it to rest. This also creates a more fragile dough. A little extra flour on the work surface and greater care will be needed when making the sgonfiotti.*

Pignolata al miele di papà
Dad's fried Easter pastry with honey

Serves 6–8

Like gnocchetti fritti, *this sweet fried pasta dish is very rich and usually served in small quantities, as with biscuits or petit fours.*

500 g (1 lb 2 oz/3⅓ cups) plain
  (all-purpose) flour
100 g (3½ oz) caster (superfine)
  sugar
a pinch of fine sea salt
6 x 55 g (2 oz) free-range
  or organic eggs
good quality vegetable oil, for frying
250 ml (9 fl oz/1 cup) honey

Combine the flour, sugar and sea salt on a work surface or large wooden board. The flour should form a peaked mound. With your hand, make a hole in the top of the mound so that it resembles a volcano. This hole needs to be big enough to be able to 'house' the eggs. Break the eggs into the hole. With your hand or with a fork, gently beat the eggs, then slowly incorporate the flour into the egg mixture. I do this by moving my hand in a circular motion, slowly incorporating the flour from the inside wall of the mound. Don't worry if the dough looks like a mess. This is normal. Once fully combined, knead a little more flour into the dough if it feels a little wet and sticky. Set the dough aside and clean the work space. Dust some fresh flour onto the work surface and continue kneading the dough for another 5 minutes. Allow the dough to rest.

Roll the dough into a 1.5 cm (⅝ inch) log, then cut it into small pieces. Roll these pieces into balls about the size of small chickpeas. Heat the vegetable oil in a deep frying pan to 180°C (350°F) and shallow-fry the balls in batches for 4 minutes or until golden. Drain on a paper towel. Allow to cool completely.

Gently heat the honey so that it becomes a thin liquid, then fold it through the pastry balls. Allow to cool, letting the honey coat the pastry. It will have a runny, toffee-like consistency.

Ravioli dolci alla calabrese

Calabrian sweet chickpea ravioli

Serves 6 (makes approximately 50 ravioli)

300 g (10½ oz/1½ cups) dried
   chickpeas, soaked in water
   overnight
100 ml (3½ fl oz) vino cotto
100 g (3½ oz) dark chocolate
   (50–60% cocoa), chopped
a pinch of fine sea salt
500 g (1 lb 2 oz/3⅓ cups) plain
   (all-purpose) flour
80 g (2¾ oz) sugar
5 x 55 g (2 oz) free-range
   or organic eggs
2½ tablespoons extra virgin olive oil
olive oil, for deep-frying
icing (confectioners') sugar,
   for dusting

Drain the chickpeas, place in a saucepan and cover with salted water. Cook until very tender. Strain, discarding the skins, and pass through a sieve.

Using a double boiler, heat the vino cotto, chocolate and sea salt over low heat until the chocolate has melted. Add the chickpea mixture and stir until the mixture is smooth. Set aside and allow to cool to room temperature.

Prepare the dough by combining the flour and the sugar on a work surface or large wooden board. The flour should form a peaked mound. With your hand, make a hole in the top of the mound so that it resembles a volcano. This hole needs to be big enough to be able to 'house' the eggs. Break the eggs into the hole and add the extra virgin olive oil. With your hand or with a fork, gently beat the eggs and oil, then slowly incorporate the flour into the egg mixture. I do this by moving my hand in a circular motion, slowly incorporating the flour from the inside wall of the mound. Don't worry if the dough looks like a mess. This is normal. Once fully combined, knead a little more flour into the dough if it feels a little wet and sticky. Set the dough aside and clean the work space. Dust some fresh flour onto the work surface and continue kneading the dough for another 5 minutes. Allow to rest for about 1 hour.

To make the ravioli, roll out the dough on a lightly floured work surface to about 2 mm (1/16 inch) in thickness and cut into round discs roughly 10 cm (4 inches) in diameter using a pastry cutter. Place a spoonful of chickpea mixture on each of the discs and fold over to the edge to form half-moons, making sure to remove as much air as possible. Press the edges down with a fork and trim with a slightly smaller cutter. Re-roll offcuts if desired.

Heat the olive oil in a deep saucepan, no more than half full, to 180°C (350°F). Deep-fry the ravioli in batches for 4 minutes or until golden brown. Drain on a paper towel and serve dusted with the icing sugar.

Ricette di Base

Base Recipes

Brodo di pollo
Chicken broth

Makes approximately 2.5 litres (87 fl oz/10 cups)

1–1.2 kg (2 lb 4 oz–2 lb 10 oz)
 free-range chicken or boiling hen
1 kg (2 lb 4 oz) fresh chicken bones,
 thoroughly washed
100 g (3½ oz) carrot, roughly
 chopped
100 g (3½ oz) celery stalks, roughly
 chopped
100 g (3½ oz) leek, roughly chopped
100 g (3½ oz) onion, roughly chopped
100 g (3½ oz) Parmigiano Reggiano
 cheese rind
3 flat-leaf (Italian) parsley sprigs
4 litres (140 fl oz/16 cups) water
fine sea salt, to taste

Place all the ingredients in a large saucepan and bring to the boil. Lower the heat and simmer without a lid for 2½–3 hours. Skim away the excess fat and other particles that come to the surface of the liquid throughout the cooking process. Remove the chicken, shred the meat from the bones (discard the skin and bones) strain the liquid through a fine strainer and refrigerate. If there is excess fat, it will solidify at the top of the refrigerated broth. Remove this with a spoon before using the broth. The cooked chicken can be used in recipes such as *Meat tortellini with classic bolognaise sauce* (page 93). Chicken broth can be made in advance and frozen in an airtight container for up to 2 months.

Brodo di pesce
Fish broth

Makes approximately 3.5 litres (122 fl oz/14 cups)

3 tablespoons olive oil
100 g (3½ oz) carrot, roughly chopped
100 g (3½ oz) celery stalks, roughly chopped
100 g (3½ oz) onion, roughly chopped
100 g (3½ oz) leek, roughly chopped
2 kg (4 lb 8 oz) fresh snapper bones (including heads),
    washed thoroughly and roughly chopped
100 ml (3½ fl oz) dry white wine
4 litres (140 fl oz/16 cups) water
2 bay leaves
5 black peppercorns
3 flat-leaf (Italian) parsley sprigs
fine sea salt, to taste

Heat the olive oil in a large saucepan over medium heat. Place all the vegetables in the saucepan and sauté until the onion and leek are soft and translucent. Add the fish bones and sauté for about 5 minutes before adding the wine. Cook until the wine has evaporated then add the water, bay leaves, peppercorns, parsley and sea salt. Bring to the boil. Lower the heat and slowly simmer without a lid for 40 minutes. Skim away the excess fat and other particles that come to the surface of the liquid throughout the cooking process. Discard the larger fish bones and strain the liquid through a fine strainer. Strain again through a fine sieve or with muslin (cheese cloth) to make sure all bones are removed and refrigerate. Fish broth can be made in advance and frozen in an airtight container for up to 2 months.

Brodo di coda di bue
Oxtail broth

Makes approximately 2.5 litres (87 fl oz/10 cups)
Yields approximately 500 g (1 lb 2 oz) oxtail meat

75 ml (2¼ fl oz) extra virgin olive oil
100 g (3½ oz) carrot, roughly chopped
100 g (3½ oz) celery stalks, roughly chopped
100 g (3½ oz) onion, roughly chopped
100 g (3½ oz) leek, roughly chopped
2 kg (4 lb 8 oz) fresh oxtail, cleaned, trimmed of excess
    fat and cut roughly into 4 cm (1½ inch) long pieces
2 ripe tomatoes, roughly chopped
3 flat-leaf (Italian) parsley sprigs
3 thyme sprigs
1 small bay leaf
4 litres (140 fl oz/16 cups) water
fine sea salt, to taste

Heat half of the extra virgin olive oil in a deep heavy-based frying pan over medium heat and sauté the carrot, celery, onion and leek until they are nicely browned. Transfer to a large saucepan. In the same frying pan, use the remaining extra virgin olive oil to sauté the oxtail until it is browned.

Add the browned oxtail and the remaining ingredients to the large saucepan and bring to the boil. Lower the heat and slowly simmer without a lid for 3–4 hours or until the meat is falling off the bone. Skim away the excess fat and other particles that come to the surface of the liquid throughout the cooking process. Take the oxtail out and set aside. Strain the liquid through a fine strainer and refrigerate. If there is excess fat, it will solidify at the top of the refrigerated broth. Remove this with a spoon and discard before using the broth. Pick the meat from the bones, discarding any fat or sinew, and reserve for later use in recipes such as *Oxtail broth with fresh pasta squares and dried wild forest mushrooms* (page 144). Oxtail broth can be made in advance and frozen in an airtight container for up to 2 months.

Brodo di vegetali
Vegetable broth

Makes approximately 3 litres (105 fl oz/12 cups)

200 g (7 oz) parsnip, roughly chopped
200 g (7 oz) turnip, roughly chopped
300 g (10½ oz) carrot, roughly chopped
100 g (3½ oz) fennel bulb, roughly chopped
300 g (10½ oz) celery stalks, roughly chopped
200 g (7 oz) leek, roughly chopped
200 g (7 oz) onion, roughly chopped
1 bay leaf
2 thyme sprigs
2 flat-leaf (Italian) parsley sprigs
5 black peppercorns
4 litres (140 fl oz/16 cups) water

Place all the ingredients in a large saucepan and bring to the boil. Lower the heat and slowly simmer for 30–60 minutes. Strain through a fine sieve and refrigerate. Vegetable broth can be made in advance and frozen in an airtight container for up to 2 months.

Brodo di manzo
Beef broth

Makes approximately 2.5 litres (87 fl oz/10 cups)

2 kg (4 lb 8 oz) beef bones and trimmings (see Note)
2 tablespoons olive oil
100 g (3½ oz) onion, roughly chopped
100 g (3½ oz) carrot, roughly chopped
100 g (3½ oz) celery stalks, roughly chopped
40 g (1½ oz) garlic cloves, peeled and roughly chopped
4 litres (140 fl oz/16 cups) water
2 ripe tomatoes, roughly chopped
2 bay leaves
5 black peppercorns
2 thyme sprigs
2 flat-leaf (Italian) parsley sprigs

Preheat the oven to 150°C (300°F/Gas 2). Place the beef bones and trimmings in a roasting tin and bake until nicely browned (approx 1–1½ hours). Heat the olive oil in a deep heavy-based frying pan and sauté the onion, carrot, celery and garlic until they are nicely browned.

Deglaze the roasting tin with some of the water then add this with all the other ingredients to a large saucepan and bring to the boil. Lower the heat and slowly simmer without a lid for 3–4 hours. Skim away the excess fat and other particles that come to the surface of the liquid throughout the cooking process. Strain the liquid through a fine strainer and refrigerate. If there is excess fat, it will solidify at the top of the refrigerated broth. Remove this with a spoon and discard before using the broth. Beef broth can be made in advance and frozen in an airtight container for up to 2 months.

NOTE: *Replace the beef bones with veal bones to make veal stock.*

Brodo di crostacei

Crustacean broth

Makes approximately 3 litres (105 fl oz/12 cups)

300 g (10½ oz) prawn (shrimp) shells

3 tablespoons olive oil

2½ tablespoons extra virgin olive oil

200 g (7 oz) onion, roughly chopped

150 g (5½ oz) carrot, roughly chopped

200 g (7 oz) celery stalks, roughly chopped

40 g (1½ oz) garlic cloves, peeled and roughly chopped

200 g (7 oz) tomato paste (concentrated purée)

2 kg (4 lb 8 oz) fresh snapper bones (including heads), washed thoroughly and roughly chopped

2 whole blue swimmer crabs, cleaned and cut into quarters

100 ml (3½ fl oz) dry white wine

1.2 kg (2 lb 10 oz) ripe fresh tomatoes, roughly chopped

3.5 litres (122 fl oz/14 cups) water

Preheat the oven to 180°C (350°F/Gas 4). Place the prawn shells in a small roasting tin and toss with the olive oil. Roast for 10–15 minutes or until golden, stirring occasionally.

In a large saucepan, heat the extra virgin olive oil over medium–high heat and add the roughly chopped vegetables and garlic. Add the roasted prawn shells and tomato paste and sauté for 1 minute. Add the snapper bones and blue swimmer crabs and sauté for about 5 minutes before adding the dry white wine. Cook until the wine has evaporated then add the tomatoes and water. Bring the stock to the boil then reduce to a slow simmer and cook for 40–60 minutes, skimming occasionally. Discard the larger fish bones and strain the liquid through a fine strainer. Make sure you press the prawn shells while straining as extra flavour is stored in them. Strain again through a fine sieve or muslin (cheese cloth) to make sure all bones are removed and refrigerate. Crustacean broth can be made in advance and frozen in an airtight container for up to 2 months.

Sugo alla napoletana
Neapolitan tomato sauce

Makes approximately 700 ml (24 fl oz)

1 garlic clove
100 ml (3½ fl oz) extra virgin olive oil
700 ml (24 fl oz) tomato purée made from
  very ripe tomatoes (see Note)
fine sea salt, to taste
6 sweet basil leaves

Crush the garlic clove under the blade of a kitchen knife, taking care to leave it in one piece. Heat the extra virgin olive oil in a saucepan to a low heat and add the garlic. Slowly cook the garlic until golden in colour and then discard. Stir in the tomato purée and season with the sea salt. Simmer for 20 minutes before adding the basil leaves.

NOTE: *Depending on the variety and ripeness, you will need up to 1.5 kg (3 lb 5 oz) whole tomatoes to yield this quantity. Please note that the quality of your tomato purée is essential. It must be made from very ripe tomatoes to ensure their sweetness. If tomatoes are not to the desired sweetness, a little sugar can be added to replace the natural sweetness of the tomatoes, but the flavour will not be the same.*

To peel and deseed the tomatoes, score a cross in the base of the tomatoes, plunge them into boiling water and then transfer to a bowl of iced water. Peel, core and squeeze out seeds. Pulse in a food processor until puréed, but be careful not to overprocess.

Ragù modenese
Modenese sauce

Makes 700 g (1 lb 9 oz)

50 g (1¾ oz) strutto (see Note)
1 celery stalk, finely diced
1 medium carrot, finely diced
1 small onion, finely diced
1 bay leaf
1 garlic clove, finely chopped
fine sea salt, to taste
freshly ground black pepper, to taste
50 g (1¾ oz) minced (ground) Italian pancetta or lardo
50 g (1¾ oz) minced (ground) cured Italian sausage,
  such as cacciatore
100 g (3½ oz) minced (ground) veal
100 g (3½ oz) minced (ground) pork
100 g (3½ oz) minced (ground) beef
250 ml (9 fl oz/1 cup) good-quality tomato passata
  (puréed tomatoes)
50 g (1¾ oz) tomato paste (concentrated purée)
250 ml (9 fl oz/1 cup) beef broth (page 187)

Heat the strutto in a saucepan and sauté the vegetables, bay leaf and garlic over medium heat until tender. Season with the sea salt and black pepper. Add the pancetta, Italian sausage and other minced meats. Cook over high heat, continually stirring, until the meat is broken into small pieces. Continue to cook, stirring until the meat is well browned and the juices have evaporated. Add the tomato passata, tomato paste and beef broth and bring to the boil. Reduce the heat to a simmer, cover and cook for 2 hours, stirring occasionally to prevent the sauce sticking to the pan. Once the sauce is cooked, remove from the saucepan and refrigerate.

NOTE: *Strutto is rendered pork lard. Nowadays, strutto is often substituted with olive oil or with a combination of olive oil and butter.*

Salsa besciamella

Béchamel sauce

Makes approximately 850 ml (29½ fl oz)

650 ml (22½ fl oz) full-cream
(whole) milk
325 ml (11 fl oz) pouring (whipping)
cream
65 g (2¼ oz) salted butter, chopped
65 g (2¼ oz) plain (all-purpose) flour
20 g (¾ oz) freshly grated Parmigiano
Reggiano cheese
1¼ teaspoon fine sea salt

Place the milk and cream in a saucepan over high heat and bring to the boil. In the meantime, you can make the *roux*. To do this, melt the butter in a separate saucepan over low heat. Take off the heat, add the flour and mix with a wooden spoon until well combined. Return the saucepan to the heat and stir continuously for 1 minute. Add the hot milk in stages, stirring at each stage until the mixture is smooth. Once all of the milk is added, add the Parmigiano Reggiano cheese and salt. Cook over low heat for approximately 10 minutes or until the sauce thickens and coats the back of a wooden spoon. Pass through a sieve to ensure any lumps are removed. Cool the bechamel to room temperature, cover the surface with plastic wrap and refrigerate if not being used straight away.

Ragù bolognese
Bolognaise sauce

Makes 850 g (1 lb 14 oz)

70 ml (2¼ fl oz) extra virgin
  olive oil

70 g (2½ oz) butter

1 celery stalk, finely diced

1 medium carrot, finely diced

1 medium brown onion, finely diced

1 bay leaf, torn

1 garlic clove, finely diced

fine sea salt, to taste

freshly ground black pepper, to taste

200 g (7 oz) mince (ground) pork

200 g (7 oz) mince (ground) veal

130 g (4½ oz) prosciutto trimmings,
  finely chopped (see Note)

100 ml (3½ oz) dry red wine

200 ml (7 fl oz) good-quality tomato
  passata (puréed tomatoes)

1 tablespoon tomato paste
  (concentrated purée)

200 ml (7 fl oz) beef broth (page 187)

Heat the extra virgin olive oil and butter in a large saucepan and sauté the vegetables, bay leaf and garlic over medium heat until tender. Season with the sea salt and black pepper. Add the pork mince, veal mince and prosciutto to the pan. Cook over high heat, stirring continuously, until the meat has broken down into small pieces. Continue to cook, stirring until the meat is well browned and the juices have evaporated. Stir in the wine and cook until it has also evaporated. Add the tomato passata, tomato paste and beef broth and bring to the boil. Reduce the heat to a simmer, cover and cook for 2 hours, stirring occasionally to prevent the sauce sticking to the pan. Once the sauce is cooked, remove from the saucepan and refrigerate until required.

NOTE: *I like to use the short/shank end of the prosciutto for this as it is difficult to slice and often gets used in other recipes that require minced or chopped prosciutto.*

Pasta fresca all'novo
Fresh egg pasta dough
Makes approximately 600 g (1 lb 5 oz)

330 g (11½ oz) plain (all-purpose)
    flour, plus extra, for kneading
70 g (2½ oz) fine semolina
½ teaspoon fine sea salt
4 x 59 g (2¼ oz) free-range
    or organic eggs

Combine the flour, semolina and sea salt and place on a work surface or large wooden board. The flour should form a peaked mound. With your hand, make a hole in the top of the mound so that it resembles a volcano. This hole needs to be big enough to be able to 'house' the eggs. Break the eggs into the hole. With your hand or with a fork, gently beat the eggs, then slowly incorporate the flour into the egg mixture. I do this by moving my hand in a circular motion, slowly incorporating the flour from the inside wall of the mound. Don't worry if the dough looks like a mess. This is normal. Once fully combined, knead a little more flour into the dough if it feels a little wet and sticky. Set the dough aside and clean the work space. Dust some fresh flour onto the work surface and continue kneading the dough for another 5 minutes. Wrap the dough in plastic and set aside in the refrigerator for at least 30 minutes. Next, roll the pasta to the desired thickness and cut into the desired shape (see pages 198–201).

Rolling & cutting the pasta dough

To roll 600 g (1 lb 5 oz) of fresh egg pasta dough, cut the rested dough into six equally sized pieces. Each piece should be roughly 100 g (3½ oz). Flatten each piece with the ends of your fingers and the palm of your hand, then commence passing the dough through a pasta machine, starting with the widest setting and then slowly reducing the width. This will make the pasta sheets increasingly thinner as you go. The pasta sheets will appear quite rough at first, but as you pass the sheets through the machine, they will become increasingly smoother. Pass the pasta through the machine at each setting at least twice.

After about the third setting, it's a good idea to fold the pasta and pass it through the machine several more times as it needs to be quite smooth. Folding also helps to create a flat edge to the pasta, and as you fold and pass it through, make sure that the dough is as wide as the rollers. This is especially important when pasta sheets are to be used for baked or filled pasta. Throughout this process, it is important to dust the pasta sheets with a little extra flour. If the dough feels wet, increase the amount of flour used to dust the sheets. This will help make a drier dough.

Once you have achieved the desired thickness, check for how moist the pasta feels. For filled pasta, moister dough is better as it helps when bending and twisting filled pasta shapes. With practice, you will become an expert at judging this. For flat pasta, such as pappardelle, tagliatelle, linguini and spaghetti, it is important to dry the pasta sheets a little prior to cutting them. This could take anywhere between 5 and 45 minutes, depending on the humidity level, air temperature and other weather conditions. If the pasta sheet is cut while too wet, the pasta strips will stick together while they are drying or cooking. At the same time, be careful not to allow the pasta to dry out too much as it will break when cut.

Filled pasta should always be stored in the refrigerator as the filling will not last long without refrigeration. At any rate, fresh filled pasta should be cooked and eaten within a day, or two days at the very most. It can be frozen, too, but fresh is always best with filled pasta. There are various methods for storing filled pasta in the refrigerator, but the best way for home use is to store with abundant loose semolina flour, which will stop the pieces sticking together, and then placing plastic wrap over and between layers. Simply dust the semolina off the pasta before cooking.

Fresh flat pasta is also best eaten soon after it is made. Remember, the longer it dries after cutting, the longer the cooking time. Storing it in the refrigerator can be complicated at home, so my suggestion is to dry it completely if you do not intend to cook and eat it straight away. This can be done by letting it dry on wooden boards or any kind of kitchen tray. Dried pasta can be stored at ambient temperature for several weeks and will be fantastic even after that period of time.

The most basic pasta machines include cutting attachments for tagliolini and fettucine, and other attachments are sold (or included with some machines) for other types of pasta. Widths vary significantly from region to region and even town to town Here is an approximate guide to:

capellini	1–2 mm (¹⁄₃₂ inch) wide
spaghetti	2 mm (³⁄₃₂ inch) wide
tagliolini	2 mm (³⁄₃₂ inch) wide
linguine	4 mm (⁵⁄₃₂ inch) wide
tagliatelle	6 mm (³⁄₈ inch) wide
fettuccine	8 mm (¼ inch) wide
pappardelle	30 mm (1¼ inch) wide

For pappardelle, if you are unable to source an attachment, you can follow this method: Lightly dust the pasta sheet with flour and shape the pasta sheet into a loose roll by folding it several times, keeping the sides straight as you fold; cut into 3 cm (1¼ inch) thick strips using a large sharp knife, then carefully unravel the pasta.

Pasta fresca di castagne

Chestnut fresh egg pasta dough

Makes approximately 600 g (1 lb 5 oz)

200 g (7 oz) chestnut flour (see Note)
200 g (7 oz/1⅓ cups) plain (all-purpose) flour,
   plus extra, for kneading
½ teaspoon fine sea salt
4 x 59 g (2¼ oz) free-range or organic eggs

Combine the flours and sea salt and place on a work surface or large wooden board. The flour should form a peaked mound. With your hand, make a hole in the top of the mound so that it resembles a volcano. This hole needs to be big enough to be able to 'house' the eggs. Break the eggs into the hole. With your hand or with a fork, gently beat the eggs, then slowly incorporate the flour into the egg mixture. I do this by moving my hand in a circular motion, slowly incorporating the flour from the inside wall of the mound. Don't worry if the dough looks like a mess. This is normal. Once fully combined, knead a little more flour into the dough if it feels a little wet and sticky. Set the dough aside and clean the work space. Dust some fresh flour onto the work surface and continue kneading the dough for another 5 minutes. Wrap the dough in plastic wrap and set aside in the refrigerator for at least 30 minutes. Next, roll the pasta to the desired thickness and cut into the desired shape (see pages 198–201).

NOTE: *Chestnut flour is available from specialty food stores.*

Pasta fresca di patate

Fresh egg potato dough

Makes approximately 600 g (1 lb 5 oz)

250 g (9 oz) whole starchy potatoes (such as bintje,
   nicola or pink-eye potatoes)
350 g (12 oz/2⅓ cups) plain (all-purpose) flour,
   plus extra, for kneading
1 teaspoon fine sea salt
2 x 59 g (2¼ oz) free-range or organic eggs

To prepare the potatoes, boil them with the skin on until soft. Peel the skin while still hot and pass the potatoes through a food mill or potato ricer. You should yield 180 g (6¼ oz) of potato.

Combine the flour, prepared potatoes and sea salt to form a crumbly mixture and place on a work surface or large wooden board. The flour mixture should form a peaked mound. With your hand, make a hole in the top of the mound so that it resembles a volcano. This hole needs to be big enough to be able to 'house' the eggs. It is a good idea to beat the eggs separately and gradually add into the hole as the potatoes may have retained extra water, requiring less egg in the mixture. With your hand or a fork, slowly incorporate the flour and potatoes into the egg mixture. I do this by moving my hand in a circular motion, slowly incorporating the flour from the inside wall of the mound. Don't worry if the dough looks like a mess. This is normal. Once fully combined, knead a little more flour into the dough if it feels a little wet and sticky. Set the dough aside and clean the work space. Dust some fresh flour onto the work surface and continue kneading the dough for another 5 minutes (see Note). Wrap the dough in plastic wrap and set aside in the refrigerator for at least 30 minutes. Next, roll the pasta to the desired thickness and cut into the desired shape (see pages 198–201).

NOTE: *Due to the lack of gluten in the potatoes, this dough will need to be kneaded a little longer to achieve the thickness required for ravioli.*

Pizzoccheri

Buckwheat fresh egg pasta

Makes approximately 600 g (1 lb 5 oz)

200 g (7 oz) buckwheat flour (see Note)
200 g (7 oz/1⅓ cups) plain (all-purpose) flour,
    plus extra, for kneading
½ teaspoon fine sea salt
4 x 59 g (2¼ oz) free-range or organic eggs

Combine the flours and sea salt and place on a work surface or large wooden board. The flour should form a peaked mound. With your hand, make a hole in the top of the mound so that it resembles a volcano. This hole needs to be big enough to be able to 'house' the eggs. Break the eggs into the hole. With your hand or with a fork, gently beat the eggs, then slowly incorporate the flour into the egg mixture. I do this by moving my hand in a circular motion, slowly incorporating the flour from the inside wall of the mound. Don't worry if the dough looks like a mess. This is normal. Once fully combined, knead a little more flour into the dough if it feels a little wet and sticky. Set the dough aside and clean the work space. Dust some fresh flour onto the work surface and continue kneading the dough for another 5 minutes. Wrap the dough in plastic wrap and set aside in the refrigerator for at least 30 minutes. Next, roll the pasta to the desired thickness and cut into fettuccine-width pasta lengths of about 6–8 cm (2½ –3¼ inches).

NOTE: *This recipe can be made with a higher ratio of buckwheat flour but it can become increasingly harder to knead.*

Pasta fresca di farro

Spelt fresh egg pasta dough

Makes approximately 600 g (1 lb 5 oz)

330 g (11½ oz) spelt flour, plus extra, for kneading
70 g (2½ oz) fine semolina
½ teaspoon fine sea salt
4 x 59 g (2¼ oz) free-range or organic eggs

Combine the spelt flour, semolina and sea salt and place on a work surface or large wooden board. The flour should form a peaked mound. With your hand, make a hole in the top of the mound so that it resembles a volcano. This hole needs to be big enough to be able to 'house' the eggs. Break the eggs into the hole. With your hand or with a fork, gently beat the eggs, then slowly incorporate the flour into the egg mixture. I do this by moving my hand in a circular motion, slowly incorporating the flour from the inside wall of the mound. Don't worry if the dough looks like a mess. This is normal. Once fully combined, knead a little more flour into the dough if it feels a little wet and sticky. Set the dough aside and clean the work space. Dust some fresh flour onto the work surface and continue kneading the dough for another 5 minutes. Wrap the dough in plastic wrap and set aside in the refrigerator for at least 30 minutes. Next, roll the pasta to the desired thickness and cut into the desired shape (see pages 198–201).

Pasta fresca alle ortiche

Stinging nettle fresh egg pasta dough

Makes approximately 600 g (1 lb 5 oz)

135 g (4¾ oz) picked stinging nettle
　leaves (see Note)
330 g (11½ oz) plain (all-purpose)
　flour, plus extra, for kneading
70 g (2½ oz) fine semolina
½ teaspoon fine sea salt
4 x 59 g (2¼ oz) free-range
　or organic eggs

NOTE: *You will need
about 450 g (1 lb) nettles
to yield this. It is a good
idea to use surgical gloves
to pick the nettles. This
recipe can also be modified
and made with any green
leafy vegetables, such as
spinach, cavolo nero, cime
di rapa, chicory, etc. Be
very careful to adequately
clean the stinging nettle or
any alternative green leafy
vegetable so as to avoid any
soil or dirt particles making
their way into the dough.*

To prepare the stinging nettles, blanch the leaves in boiling water for 2 minutes then refresh in iced water. Strain the stinging nettle and squeeze as much liquid out as you can. This can be achieved by wringing out the nettle in a clean tea towel (dish towel). Place the nettle into a mortar and, using a pestle, work it until it is finely ground. It can also be blended in a food processor, but if overworked it will turn your dough a fluorescent green.

Combine the flour, semolina and sea salt and place on a work surface or large wooden board. The flour should form a peaked mound. With your hand, make a hole in the top of the mound so that it resembles a volcano. This hole needs to be big enough to be able to 'house' the eggs. Break the eggs into the hole and add the prepared nettles. With your hand or with a fork, gently beat the eggs, then slowly incorporate the flour into the egg mixture. I do this by moving my hand in a circular motion, slowly incorporating the flour from the inside wall of the mound. Don't worry if the dough looks like a mess. This is normal. Once fully combined, knead a little more flour into the dough if it feels a little wet and sticky. Set the dough aside and clean the work space. Dust some fresh flour onto the work surface and continue kneading the dough for another 5 minutes. Wrap the dough in plastic wrap and set aside in the refrigerator for at least 30 minutes. Next, roll the pasta to the desired thickness and cut into the desired shape (see pages 198–201).

Pasta fresca al nero di seppia
Squid/cuttlefish ink fresh egg pasta dough

Makes approximately 600 g (1 lb 5 oz)

330 g (11½ oz) plain (all-purpose)
   flour, plus extra, for kneading
70 g (2½ oz) fine semolina
½ teaspoon fine sea salt
3 x 59 g (2¼ oz) free-range
   or organic eggs
40 g (1½ oz) squid/cuttlefish ink
   (see Note)
1 teaspoon water

Combine the flour, semolina and sea salt and place on a work surface or large wooden board. The flour should form a peaked mound. With your hand, make a hole in the top of the mound so that it resembles a volcano. This hole needs to be big enough to be able to 'house' the eggs. Break the eggs into the hole. Combine the squid ink with the water and add to the eggs. With your hand or with a fork, gently beat the ink and egg mixture, then slowly incorporate the flour. I do this by moving my hand in a circular motion, slowly incorporating the flour from the inside wall of the mound. Don't worry if the dough looks like a mess. This is normal. Once fully combined, knead a little more flour into the dough if it feels a little wet and sticky. Set the dough aside and clean the work space. Dust some fresh flour onto the work surface and continue kneading the dough for another 5 minutes. Wrap the dough in plastic wrap and set aside in the refrigerator for at least 30 minutes. Next, roll the pasta to the desired thickness and cut into the desired shape (see pages 198–201).

NOTE: *Both squid and cuttlefish ink make good black pasta and can be substituted for each other. Ink products sold in jars are the most convenient source. However, you can obtain it from both fresh cuttlefish and squid as it is contained in the silver/black sacs inside of the fish. Extracting it will take a little practice, but it is a great source of squid or cuttlefish ink.*

Pasta fresca allo zafferano
Saffron fresh egg pasta dough
Makes approximately 600 g (1 lb 5 oz)

1½ teaspoons saffron threads

85 ml (2¾ fl oz) water

330 g (11½ oz) plain (all-purpose)
  flour, plus extra, for kneading

70 g (2½ oz) fine semolina

½ teaspoon fine sea salt

3 x 59 g (2¼ oz) free-range
  or organic eggs

Place the saffron threads and water in a small saucepan and slowly bring to a simmer. Simmer until reduced by a third. Strain, discarding the saffron threads, and cool to room temperature.

Combine the flour, semolina and sea salt and place on a work surface or large wooden board. The flour should form a peaked mound. With your hand, make a hole in the top of the mound so that it resembles a volcano. This hole needs to be big enough to be able to 'house' the eggs. Break the eggs into the hole and add the saffron reduction. With your hand or with a fork, gently beat the eggs, then slowly incorporate the flour into the egg mixture. I do this by moving my hand in a circular motion, slowly incorporating the flour from the inside wall of the mound. Don't worry if the dough looks like a mess. This is normal. Once fully combined, knead a little more flour into the dough if it feels a little wet and sticky. Set the dough aside and clean the work space. Dust some fresh flour onto the work surface and continue kneading the dough for another 5 minutes. Wrap the dough in plastic wrap and set aside in the refrigerator for at least 30 minutes. Next, roll the pasta to the desired thickness and cut into the desired shape (see pages 198–201).

Gnocchi di patate
Potato gnocchi

Makes approximately 600 g (1 lb 5 oz)

650 g (1 lb 7 oz) whole starchy
    potatoes (such as bintje, nicola
    or pink-eye potatoes)
½ beaten 59 g (2¼ oz) free-range
    or organic egg
½ teaspoon fine sea salt
150 g (5½ oz/1 cup) plain
    (all-purpose) flour

To prepare the potatoes, boil them with the skin on until soft (see Note). Peel the skin while still hot and pass through a food mill or potato ricer. You should yield about 500 g (1 lb 2 oz) of potato.

Transfer the potato to a large bowl and add the beaten egg and sea salt. Carefully work the flour into the mix, reserving 1 tablespoon for dusting. With the remaining flour, dust down a clean flat work surface and begin to roll a quarter of the dough at a time to form long sausage-like shapes approximately 1 cm (½ inch) in diameter. Cut at 1 cm (½ inch) intervals to form little dumplings. These can then be rolled over a serrated wooden gnocchi roller or the end of a fork to form small grooves. This is not necessary, but it is done so that the gnocchi will hold more sauce when served. Repeat with the rest of the dough. Using a spatula, carefully transfer to a tray lined with non-stick baking paper until ready to use.

NOTE: *It is important to ensure that the potatoes are not left in water unnecessarily as any extra water that is carried into the dough will make it too wet, requiring extra flour. With extra flour, the texture of the gnocchi becomes less soft, which is undesirable. To make good gnocchi, the idea is to use as little extra flour as possible.*

Gnocchi alla dalmatina di Ino

Ino Kuvacic's Dalmatian-style butter gnocchi

Makes approximately 600 g (1 lb 5 oz)

520 g (1 lb 2½ oz) whole starchy potatoes (such as bintje, nicola or pink-eye potatoes)

1 tablespoon beaten free-range or organic egg

40 g (1½ oz) freshly grated Parmigiano Reggiano cheese

40 g (1½ oz) butter, chopped and softened

½ teaspoon fine sea salt, to taste

100 g (3½ oz/1⅔ cups) plain (all-purpose) flour

To prepare the potatoes, boil them with the skin on until soft (see Note on page 212). Peel the skin while still hot and pass through a food mill or potato ricer. You should yield about 400 g (14 oz) of potato.

Transfer the potato to a large bowl and add the beaten egg, Parmigiano Reggiano cheese, butter and sea salt. Carefully work the flour into the mix, reserving 1 tablespoon for dusting. With the remaining flour, dust down a clean flat work surface and begin to roll a quarter of the dough into a log that is 2 cm (¾ inch) in diameter. Cut at 2 cm (¾ inch) intervals. Repeat with the rest of the dough. Using a spatula, carefully transfer to a tray lined with non-stick baking paper until ready to use.

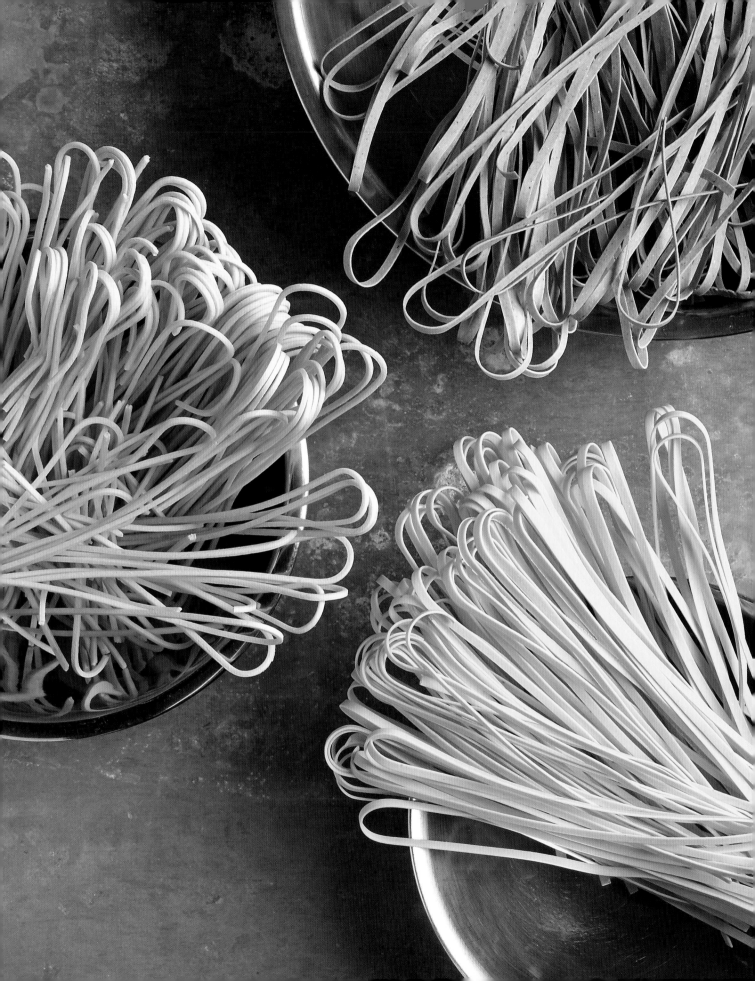

Glossario
Glossary

BAKED RICOTTA: Baked ricotta is made from cow's, sheep's or goat's milk ricotta that is oven baked until it is dry and slightly browned.

BLOOD ORANGE AGRUMATO OLIVE OIL: Agrumato olive oils are made by simultaneously grinding fresh olives with fresh citrus fruit to produce a high-quality citrus-flavoured olive oil. Blood orange agrumato olive oil has a blood orange and olive oil aroma and flavour.

BUFFALO MOZZARELLA—AGED: An aged mozzarella made from the milk of the domestic water buffalo in the Campania region of Italy. If you cannot find aged buffalo mozzarella, any aged cow's milk mozzarella or provola cheese is a suitable replacement.

BUFFALO MOZZARELLA—FRESH: A highly prized fresh mozzarella made from the milk of the domestic water buffalo in the Campania region of Italy. Buffalo mozzarella is now also made outside of the Campania region of Italy; however, its quality can be significantly inferior.

CIME DI RAPA: Cime di rapa are the clusters of green buds that resemble small heads of broccoli that surround the spiked leaves of Italian turnip greens. The leaves (also known as rapa, turnip greens or turnip tops) can be used with, or instead of, the green buds. Both have a mustardy, nutty and bitter flavour.

EMMENTAL: A yellow, medium-hard Swiss cheese that has a savoury flavour typical of Swiss cheeses. Although originally from Switzerland, emmental cheese is widely used in Italian cooking, particularly in northern Italy.

FONTINA: Fontina is a cow's milk Italian cheese that has been made in the Aosta Valley in the Italian Alps since the 12th century. It is a hard cheese with a flavour profile that can range from mild to intense (depending on its age and production), with nutty and herbaceous characteristics.

GARUM (FERMENTED FISH SAUCE): Used in Roman times, garum is a salty, pungent sauce made from fermented anchovies.

GORGONZOLA: A famous blue-veined soft cheese made from cow's and/or goat's milk. It can be creamy or firm, depending on its age, and quite salty, with a 'bite' from its blue veining. There are two kinds: Gorgonzola Piccante and Gorgonzola Dolce Latte. Piccante is more intense, with a much stronger taste and veining, and Dolce Latte is creamier. Today, the cheese is made in two Italian regions: Piedmont and Lombardy.

LARDO: Lardo is a type of *salume* (Italian charcuterie) that is made by curing strips of pork back fat (prosciutto-style) with rosemary and other herbs and spices. The most famous is made in Colonnata in Tuscany. However, good-quality cured lardo is now made all over Italy and abroad.

MOSCATO WINE: A sparkling white wine produced mainly in the province of Asti in north-west Italy. Sweet and low in alcohol, it is made from the Moscato Bianco grape.

MOSTO COTTO (VINO COTTO): Mosto cotto is made from the must or juice of freshly pressed premium dark wine grapes. The must is slowly cooked and reduced to a syrup. It can be used immediately or cellared for many months or even years. With cellaring, the flavour will naturally intensify over time. It is used extensively in desserts and cakes.

MUSTARD FRUITS: Originating in Cremona in Italy, mustard fruits are made by preserving different fruits in a sweet, viscous, mustard-flavoured syrup.

'NDUJA SAUSAGE: A very spicy, spreadable Calabrian salami that can be made from various pork cuts, such as shoulder, belly, jowl and tripe. It also contains a mixture of spices as well as chillies that are boiled then roasted dry before being added to the meat, which gives the sausage a very paprika-like flavour.

RICOTTA FRESCA (FRESH RICOTTA): A soft, sweet, white curd cheese made from cow, sheep, goat or buffalo milk, or any combination of these milks. It is widely used in Italian cooking, particularly in baked pasta, filled pasta and desserts.

RICOTTA SALATA (SALTED DRIED RICOTTA): Ricotta salata is fresh ricotta that has been pressed, salted, dried and aged for 2–4 months. Ricotta salata is hard and white, with a salty, nutty and milky flavour. It can be shaved or grated over salads, pastas and vegetable dishes.

SCAMORZA: An Italian cheese similar to aged mozzarella or provola. It is often smoked and exhibits a mild, smoky flavour. Predominantly made from cow's milk, it can also be made from other types of milk. Sheep's milk scamorza, for instance, is a traditional product of Puglia.

SCORZANERA (BLACK SALSIFY): Similar to a carrot in shape, scorzanera or black salsify is one of the more uncommon root vegetables. Black salsify differs to regular salsify in that it has a black skin as opposed to beige-white. Both have the same flavour, but the black variety is much more prevalent in Italy.

SQUID/CUTTLEFISH INK OR NERO DI SEPPIA: A naturally occurring black ink found in small sacs inside squid and cuttlefish. It is used as a condiment, flavouring and/or colouring in various Italian dishes. The ink can be used fresh or bought in jars at specialty food stores.

STINGING NETTLES: A green, weed-like plant with hollow, stinging hairs on its leaves and stems. When touched by humans or animals it can inject chemicals that produce a stinging sensation. Stinging nettles must be handled with gloves, but once cooked (or blanched) they no longer produce their sting. The plant has a long history as a medicine and food source.

STRUTTO: Strutto is rendered pork lard. Nowadays, strutto is often substituted with other cooking fats, such as olive oil or a combination of olive oil and butter.

TRUFFLE—BLACK: *Tuber melanosporum* or black truffle is the fruiting body of an underground mushroom that grows symbiotically within the root system of trees, predominantly oak and hazelnut. Thoroughly black in colour (unlike the inferior black summer truffle, which has a black skin and cream-coloured inside), it is highly prized for its unique flavour and aroma.

TRUFFLE—WHITE (ALBA): *Tuber magnatum* or white Alba truffle (also locally known in Italy as the *Alba madonna*) is the fruiting body of an underground mushroom that grows symbiotically within the root system of trees, predominantly oak, hazelnut, poplar and beech. Thoroughly cream in colour and mainly found in and around the town of Alba in northern Italy, it is the most expensive and highly prized of all truffles because of the uniqueness of its flavour and aroma.

Indice
Index

Acknowledgments

There are a lot of people who I need to thank. Firstly, my father, without whom this book would have no reference. Even at the age of 76 he is the most active and productive person I know. His cellar, his vineyard, his garden and his kitchen are a constant source of gastronomic inspiration and wisdom. Thanks to my mother, for her independent voice and passion for people, food and culture. To my two brothers with big hearts, Paul and Ross, who have put up with my over-enthusiasm for everything for most of their lives. To my extended family of uncles, aunties and cousins in Australia, Italy and France, for their enormous support and generosity throughout my life. They are special people—all of them.

A very special thanks to Liliana Di Certo and Ottavio Zoccali in Calabria, for their bountiful support. Thanks also to Carmela Greco for her kindness and generosity of spirit. To Professor John Scott from the University of Western Australia, for arousing an interest in Italian language and high culture in an unlikely enthusiast. To all of the Syrmis family, for the kind of unconditional support one can only dream possible from in-laws. They are the most generous and supportive people I know. To the chefs and colleagues who have helped me along the way, relationships that in some part 'stay with you even when they don't stay with you': Owen Trott, Russell Barr, Peter Martini, Michael Wise, Vince Garreffa, Khan Danis, Catherine Adams, Ino Kuvacic, Maurizio Terzini, Clive Kitchen, Mark Beattie, Mitch Edwards, the Seidel family, Margi Kirby and many, many more. To Robert Armstrong and Faithfull. To past and present Pendolino staff who have played a big role in making 'pasta' the centre stage of the restaurant. In particular, to Vasilios Donoudis, Ciro Montuori, Felicity Goodall, Chris Campbell, Luukas Trautner, Lachlan Robinson, Sally Jackson and many more. A special thank you to sommelier Cristian Casarin for his knowledge, passion, honesty and authenticity, and to Raffaello Pignetti, a genuine hospitality gentleman and wise man in the truest sense of the word. To my publisher Murdoch Books and all the staff involved in the process.

Lastly, to Krissoula and Luca. To my wife Krissoula, who is my best friend, confidante and partner in just about everything that I do. Thank you for being yourself. And to my greatest inspiration, my son Luca, who is the smartest person I know—he is simply a gift. This book is dedicated to them.

Ringraziamenti

Sono molte le persone a cui sento il bisogno di esprimere i miei ringraziamenti. Comincerei, innanzitutto, da mio padre, la persona cioè, cui questo libro deve la sua progettazione e la sua realizzazione. Alla veneranda età di 76 anni, mio padre è un esempio incredibile di produttività e dinamicità; la sua vigna, la sua cantina, la sua cucina, sono sorgenti inesauribili di ispirazione gastronomica nonché meravigliosa espressione di saggezza contadina. Il mio grazie va poi a mia madre, voce indipendente e oggettiva, alla sua passione per la gente, per il cibo e per la cultura che a tutto ciò si richiama. Grazie anche ai miei fratelli Paul e Ross, alla loro generosità, alla loro capacità di aver sopportato il mio esuberante entusiasmo per tutta la vita. I segni della mia riconoscenza vanno poi alla parte allargata della mia famiglia: agli zii, alle zie, ai cugini in Australia, in Francia e in Italia per la loro disponibilità e l'incoraggiamento che da loro ho sempre ricevuto. Sono tutti per me molto 'speciali'.

Un grazie particolare a Liliana Di Certo ed Ottavio Zoccali che dalla Calabria non mi hanno fatto mancare il loro prezioso stimolo. Grazie anche a Carmela Greco per la sua gentilezza e generosità. Vorrei, inoltre, citare il Prof. John Scott dell'università del Western Australia per avere instillato in me l'interesse per la lingua italiana e per la cultura italiana in senso lato. Gratitudine alla famiglia Syrmis per il loro appoggio incondizionato; i miei suoceri sono stati assolutamente incomparabili nella loro generosità e nel loro sostegno. Non dimentico poi i miei colleghi che mi hanno aiutato per tutto il tempo; una presenza la loro che va ben oltre quella fisica. Cito al riguardo Owen Trott, Russell Barr, Peter Martini, Michael Wise, Vince Garreffa, Khan Danis, Catherine Adams, Ino Kuvacic, Maurizio Terzini, Clive Kitchen, Mark Beattie, Mitch Edwards, la famiglia Seidel, Margi Kirby e tanti altri ancora. Grazie inoltre a Robert Armstrong e Faithfull. Grazie a tutto il personale del Pendolino, a quello presente e a tutti coloro che ne hanno fatto parte in passato; grazie per il ruolo importante giocato nel fare della 'pasta' il fiore all'occhiello del nostro ristorante. Particolare menzione a Vasilios Donoudis, Ciro Montuori, Felicity Goodall, Chris Campbell, Luukas Trautner, Lachlan Robinson, Sally Jackson e molti altri. Uno speciale grazie al sommelier Cristian Casarin per la sua competenza, passione, onestà e autenticità. Grazie anche a Raffaello Pignetti, un genuino 'gentleman' dell'ospitalità e una persona saggia nel vero senso del termine. Ringrazio il mio editore Murdoch Books e tutto il personale coinvolto in questo lavoro.

Infine Luca e Krissoula. Grazie a mia moglie Krissoula, la mia compagna, la mia confidente, la mia complice in tutto ciò che realizzo. Grazie Krissoula per essere quello che sei! E per finire, grazie al mio più 'grande' ispiratore: mio figlio Luca, la persona più perspicace che io conosca, il dono più prezioso che la vita mi abbia fatto. È a loro che questo libro è dedicato.

Published in 2012 by Murdoch Books Pty Limited

Murdoch Books Australia
Pier 8/9
23 Hickson Road
Millers Point NSW 2000
Phone: +61 (0) 2 8220 2000
Fax: +61 (0) 2 8220 2558
www.murdochbooks.com.au
info@murdochbooks.com.au

Murdoch Books UK Limited
Erico House, 6th Floor
93–99 Upper Richmond Road
Putney, London SW15 2TG
Phone: +44 (0) 20 8785 5995
Fax: +44 (0) 20 8785 5985
www.murdochbooks.co.uk
info@murdochbooks.co.uk

For Corporate Orders & Custom Publishing contact Noel Hammond,
National Business Development Manager, Murdoch Books Australia.

Publisher: Sally Webb
Design Concept: Debra Billson
Design Layout: Emma Gough
Photographer: Nicky Ryan
Stylist: Michelle Noerianto
Project Editor: Alice Grundy
Editor: Gabriella Sterio
Food Editor: Sonia Greig
Home Economist: Olivia Andrews
Production: Joan Beal

A cataloguing-in-publication entry is available from the catalogue of the National Library
of Australia at www.nla.gov.au.

Printed by 1010 Printing International Limited, China.

The publisher and stylist would like to thank Robert Gordon Australia for lending equipment for use and photography.

IMPORTANT: Those who might be at risk from the effects of salmonella poisoning (the elderly,
pregnant women, young children and those suffering from immune deficiency diseases) should
consult their doctor with any concerns about eating raw eggs.

OVEN GUIDE: You may find cooking times vary depending on the oven you are using. For fan-forced
ovens, as a general rule, set the oven temperature to 20°C (35°F) lower than indicated in the recipe.

We have used 20 ml (4 teaspoon) tablespoon measures. If you are using a 15 ml (3 teaspoon) tablespoon
add an extra teaspoon of the ingredient for each tablespoon specified.